THE PELICAN SHAKESPEARE
GENERAL EDITORS

STEPHEN ORGEL
A. R. BRAUNMULLER

Cymbeline

Ellen Terry as Imogen, at the Lyceum, 1896

William Shakespeare

Cymbeline

EDITED BY PETER HOLLAND

PENGUIN BOOKS

PENGUIN BOOKS
Published by the Penguin Group
Penguin Group (USA) Inc., 375 Hudson Street, New York, New York 10014, U.S.A.
Penguin Books Ltd, 80 Strand, London WC2R 0RL, England
Penguin Books Australia Ltd, 250 Camberwell Road, Camberwell, Victoria 3124, Australia
Penguin Books Canada Ltd, 10 Alcorn Avenue, Toronto, Ontario, Canada M4V 3B2
Penguin Books India (P) Ltd, 11 Community Centre, Panchsheel Park, New Delhi – 110 017, India
Penguin Books (N.Z.) Ltd, Cnr Rosedale and Airborne Roads, Albany, Auckland, New Zealand
Penguin Books (South Africa) (Pty) Ltd, 24 Sturdee Avenue,
Rosebank, Johannesburg 2196, South Africa

Penguin Books Ltd, Registered Offices: 80 Strand, London WC2R 0RL, England

Cymbeline edited by Robert B. Heilman published in the
United States of America in Penguin Books 1964
Revised edition published 1979
This new edition edited by Peter Holland published 2000

9   10   8

ISBN 0-14-07.1472-3

Printed in the United States of America
Set in Garamond
Designed by Virginia Norey

Contents

Publisher's Note

IT IS ALMOST half a century since the first volumes of the Pelican Shakespeare appeared under the general editorship of Alfred Harbage. The fact that a new edition, rather than simply a revision, has been undertaken reflects the profound changes textual and critical studies of Shakespeare have undergone in the past twenty years. For the new Pelican series, the texts of the plays and poems have been thoroughly revised in accordance with recent scholarship, and in some cases have been entirely reedited. New introductions and notes have been provided in all the volumes. But the new Shakespeare is also designed as a successor to the original series; the previous editions have been taken into account, and the advice of the previous editors has been solicited where it was feasible to do so.

Certain textual features of the new Pelican Shakespeare should be particularly noted. All lines are numbered that contain a word, phrase, or allusion explained in the glossarial notes. In addition, for convenience, every tenth line is also numbered, in italics when no annotation is indicated. The intrusive and often inaccurate place headings inserted by early editors are omitted (as is becoming standard practice), but for the convenience of those who miss them, an indication of locale now appears as the first item in the annotation of each scene.

In the interest of both elegance and utility, each speech prefix is set in a separate line when the speaker's lines are in verse, except when those words form the second half of a verse line. Thus the verse form of the speech is kept visually intact. What is printed as verse and what is printed as prose has, in general, the authority of the original texts. Departures from the original texts in this regard have only the authority of editorial tradition and the judgment of the Pelican editors; and, in a few instances, are admittedly arbitrary.

The Theatrical World

ECONOMIC REALITIES determined the theatrical world in which Shakespeare's plays were written, performed, and received. For centuries in England, the primary theatrical tradition was nonprofessional. Craft guilds (or "mysteries") provided religious drama – mystery plays – as part of the celebration of religious and civic festivals, and schools and universities staged classical and neoclassical drama in both Latin and English as part of their curricula. In these forms, drama was established and socially acceptable. Professional theater, in contrast, existed on the margins of society. The acting companies were itinerant; playhouses could be any available space – the great halls of the aristocracy, town squares, civic halls, inn yards, fair booths, or open fields – and income was sporadic, dependent on the passing of the hat or on the bounty of local patrons. The actors, moreover, were considered little better than vagabonds, constantly in danger of arrest or expulsion.

In the late 1560s and 1570s, however, English professional theater began to gain respectability. Wealthy aristocrats fond of drama – the Lord Admiral, for example, or the Lord Chamberlain – took acting companies under their protection so that the players technically became members of their households and were no longer subject to arrest as homeless or masterless men. Permanent theaters were first built at this time as well, allowing the companies to control and charge for entry to their performances.

Shakespeare's livelihood, and the stunning artistic explosion in which he participated, depended on pragmatic and architectural effort. Professional theater requires ways to restrict access to its offerings; if it does not, and admission fees cannot be charged, the actors do not get paid, the costumes go to a pawnbroker, and there is no such thing as a professional, ongoing theatrical tradition. The answer to that economic need arrived in the late 1560s and 1570s with the creation of the so-called public or am-phitheater playhouse. Recent discoveries indicate that the precursor of the Globe playhouse in London (where Shakespeare's mature plays were presented) and the Rose theater (which presented Christopher Marlowe's plays and some of Shakespeare's earliest ones) was the Red Lion theater of 1567. Archaeological studies of the foundations of the Rose and Globe theaters have revealed that the open-air theater of the 1590s and later was probably a polygonal building with fourteen to twenty or twenty-four sides, multistoried, from 75 to 100 feet in diameter, with a raised, partly covered "thrust" stage that projected into a group of standing patrons, or "groundlings," and a covered gallery, seating up to 2,500 or more (very crowded) spectators.

These theaters might have been about half full on any given day, though the audiences were larger on holidays or when a play was advertised, as old and new were, through printed playbills posted around London. The metropolitan area's late-Tudor, early-Stuart population (circa 1590-1620) has been estimated at about 150,000 to 250,000. It has been supposed that in the mid-1590s there were about 15,000 spectators per week at the public theaters; thus, as many as 10 percent of the local popula-tion went to the theater regularly. Consequently, the the-aters' repertories – the plays available for this experienced and frequent audience – had to change often: in the month between September 15 and October 15, 1595, for instance, the Lord Admiral's Men performed twenty-eight times in eighteen different plays.

Since natural light illuminated the amphitheaters' stages, performances began between noon and two o'clock and ran without a break for two or three hours. They often concluded with a jig, a fencing display, or some other nondramatic exhibition. Weather conditions determined the season for the amphitheaters: plays were performed every day (including Sundays, sometimes, to clerical dismay) except during Lent – the forty days before Easter – or periods of plague, or sometimes during the summer months when law courts were not in session and the most affluent members of the audience were not in London.

To a modern theatergoer, an amphitheater stage like that of the Rose or Globe would appear an unfamiliar mixture of plainness and elaborate decoration. Much of the structure was carved or painted, sometimes to imitate marble; elsewhere, as under the canopy projecting over the stage, to represent the stars and the zodiac. Appropriate painted canvas pictures (of Jerusalem, for example, if the play was set in that city) were apparently hung on the wall behind the acting area, and tragedies were accompanied by black hangings, presumably something like crepe festoons or bunting. Although these theaters did not employ what we would call scenery, early modern spectators saw numerous large props, such as the "bar" at which a prisoner stood during a trial, the "mossy bank" where lovers reclined, an arbor for amorous conversation, a chariot, gallows, tables, trees, beds, thrones, writing desks, and so forth. Audiences might learn a scene's location from a sign (reading "Athens," for example) carried across the stage (as in Bertolt Brecht's twentieth-century productions). Equally captivating (and equally irritating to the theater's enemies) were the rich costumes and personal props the actors used: the most valuable items in the surviving theatrical inventories are the swords, gowns, robes, crowns, and other items worn or carried by the performers.

Magic appealed to Shakespeare's audiences as much as it does to us today, and the theater exploited many deceptive and spectacular devices. A winch in the loft above the stage, called "the heavens," could lower and raise actors playing gods, goddesses, and other supernatural figures to and from the main acting area, just as one or more trapdoors permitted entrances and exits to and from the area, called "hell," beneath the stage. Actors wore elementary makeup such as wigs, false beards, and face paint, and they employed pig's bladders filled with animal blood to make wounds seem more real. They had rudimentary but effective ways of pretending to behead or hang a person. Supernumeraries (stagehands or actors not needed in a particular scene) could make thunder sounds (by shaking a metal sheet or rolling an iron ball down a chute) and show lightning (by blowing inflammable resin through tubes into a flame). Elaborate fireworks enhanced the effects of dragons flying through the air or imitated such celestial phenomena as comets, shooting stars, and multiple suns. Horses' hoofbeats, bells (located perhaps in the tower above the stage), trumpets and drums, clocks, cannon shots and gunshots, and the like were common sound effects. And the music of viols, cornets, oboes, and recorders was a regular feature of theatrical performances.

For two relatively brief spans, from the late 1570s to 1590 and from 1599 to 1614, the amphitheaters competed with the so-called private, or indoor, theaters, which originated as, or later represented themselves as, educational institutions training boys as singers for church services and court performances. These indoor theaters had two features that were distinct from the amphitheaters': their personnel and their playing spaces. The amphitheaters' adult companies included both adult men, who played the male roles, and boys, who played the female roles; the private, or indoor, theater companies, on the other hand, were entirely composed of boys aged about 8 to 16, who were, or could pretend to be, candidates for singers in a church or a royal boys' choir. (Until 1660, professional theatrical companies included no women.) The playing space would appear much more familiar to modern audiences than the long-vanished amphitheaters; the later indoor theaters were, in fact, the ancestors of the typical modern theater. They were enclosed spaces, usually rectangular, with the stage filling one end of the rectangle and the audience arrayed in seats or benches across (and sometimes lining) the building's longer axis. These spaces staged plays less frequently than the public theaters (perhaps only once a week) and held far fewer spectators than the amphitheaters: about 200 to 600, as opposed to 2,500 or more. Fewer patrons mean a smaller gross income, unless each pays more. Not surprisingly, then, private theaters charged higher prices than the amphitheaters, probably sixpence, as opposed to a penny for the cheapest entry.

Protected from the weather, the indoor theaters presented plays later in the day than the amphitheaters, and used artificial illumination – candles in sconces or candelabra. But candles melt, and need replacing, snuffing, and trimming, and these practical requirements may have been part of the reason the indoor theaters introduced breaks in the performance, the intermission so dear to the heart of theatergoers and to the pocketbooks of theater concessionaires ever since. Whether motivated by the need to tend to the candles or by the entrepreneurs' wishing to sell oranges and liquor, or both, the indoor theaters eventually established the modern convention of the noncontinuous performance. In the early modern "private" theater, musical performances apparently filled the intermissions, which in Stuart theater jargon seem to have been called "acts."

At the end of the first decade of the seventeenth century, the distinction between public amphitheaters and private indoor companies ceased. For various cultural, political, and economic reasons, individual companies gained control of both the public, open-air theaters and the indoor ones, and companies mixing adult men and boys took over the formerly "private" theaters. Despite the death of the boys' companies and of their highly innovative theaters (for which such luminous playwrights as Ben Jonson, George Chapman, and John Marston wrote), their playing spaces and conventions had an immense impact on subsequent plays: not merely for the intervals (which stressed the artistic and architectonic importance of "acts"), but also because they introduced political and social satire as a popular dramatic ingredient, even in tragedy, and a wider range of actorly effects, encouraged by their more intimate playing spaces.

Even the briefest sketch of the Shakespearean theatrical world would be incomplete without some comment on the social and cultural dimensions of theaters and playing in the period. In an intensely hierarchical and status-conscious society, professional actors and their ventures had hardly any respectability; as we have indicated, to protect themselves against laws designed to curb vagabondage and the increase of masterless men, actors resorted to the near-fiction that they were the servants of noble masters, and wore their distinctive livery. Hence the company for which Shakespeare wrote in the 1590s called itself the Lord Chamberlain's Men and pretended that the public, money-getting performances were in fact rehearsals for private performances before that high court official. From 1598, the Privy Council had licensed theatrical companies, and after 1603, with the accession of King James I, the companies gained explicit royal protection, just as the Queen's Men had for a time under Queen Elizabeth. The Chamberlain's Men became the King's Men, and the other companies were patronized by the other members of the royal family.

These designations were legal fictions that half-concealed an important economic and social development, the evolution away from the theater's organization on the model of the guild, a self-regulating confraternity of individual artisans, into a proto-capitalist organization. Shakespeare's company became a joint-stock company, where persons who supplied capital and, in some cases, such as Shakespeare's, capital and talent, employed themselves and others in earning a return on that capital. This development meant that actors and theater companies were outside both the traditional guild structures, which required some form of civic or royal charter, and the feudal household organization of master-and-servant. This anomalous, maverick social and economic condition made theater companies practically unruly and potentially even dangerous; consequently, numerous official bodies – including the London metropolitan and ecclesiastical authorities as well as, occasionally, the royal court itself – tried, without much success, to control and even to disband them.

Public officials had good reason to want to close the theaters: they were attractive nuisances – they drew often riotous crowds, they were always noisy, and they could be politically offensive and socially insubordinate. Until the Civil War, however, anti-theatrical forces failed to shut down professional theater, for many reasons – limited surveillance and few police powers, tensions or outright hostilities among the agencies that sought to check or channel theatrical activity, and lack of clear policies for control. Another reason must have been the theaters' undeniable popularity. Curtailing any activity enjoyed by such a substantial percentage of the population was difficult, as various Roman emperors attempting to limit circuses had learned, and the Tudor-Stuart audience was not merely large, it was socially diverse and included women. The prevalence of public entertainment in this period has been underestimated. In fact, fairs, holidays, games, sporting events, the equivalent of modern parades, freak shows, and street exhibitions all abounded, but the theater was the most widely and frequently available entertainment to which people of every class had access. That fact helps account both for its quantity and for the fear and anger it aroused.

WILLIAM SHAKESPEARE OF
STRATFORD-UPON-AVON, GENTLEMAN

Many people have said that we know very little about
William Shakespeare's life – pinheads and postcards are
often mentioned as appropriately tiny surfaces on which
to record the available information. More imaginatively
and perhaps more correctly, Ralph Waldo Emerson wrote,
"Shakespeare is the only biographer of Shakespeare. . . .
So far from Shakespeare's being the least known, he is the
one person in all modern history fully known to us."

In fact, we know more about Shakespeare's life than we
do about almost any other English writer's of his era. His
last will and testament (dated March 25, 1616) survives,
as do numerous legal contracts and court documents involving Shakespeare as principal or witness, and parish
records in Stratford and London. Shakespeare appears
quite often in official records of King James's royal court,
and of course Shakespeare's name appears on numerous
title pages and in the written and recorded words of his
literary contemporaries Robert Greene, Henry Chettle,
Francis Meres, John Davies of Hereford, Ben Jonson, and
many others. Indeed, if we make due allowance for the
bloating of modern, run-of-the-mill bureaucratic records,
more information has survived over the past four hundred
years about William Shakespeare of Stratford-upon-Avon,
Warwickshire, than is likely to survive in the next four
hundred years about any reader of these words.

What we do not have are entire categories of information – Shakespeare's private letters or diaries, drafts and
revisions of poems and plays, critical prefaces or essays,
commendatory verse for other writers' works, or instructions guiding his fellow actors in their performances, for
instance – that we imagine would help us understand and
appreciate his surviving writings. For all we know, many
such data never existed as written records. Many literary

and theatrical critics, not knowing what might once have existed, more or less cheerfully accept the situation; some even make a theoretical virtue of it by claiming that such data are irrelevant to understanding and interpreting the plays and poems.

So, what do we know about William Shakespeare, the man responsible for thirty-seven or perhaps more plays, more than 150 sonnets, two lengthy narrative poems, and some shorter poems?

While many families by the name of Shakespeare (or some variant spelling) can be identified in the English Midlands as far back as the twelfth century, it seems likely that the dramatist's grandfather, Richard, moved to Snitterfield, a town not far from Stratford-upon-Avon, sometime before 1529. In Snitterfield, Richard Shakespeare leased farmland from the very wealthy Robert Arden. By 1552, Richard's son John had moved to a large house on Henley Street in Stratford-upon-Avon, the house that stands today as "The Birthplace." In Stratford, John Shakespeare traded as a glover, dealt in wool, and lent money at interest; he also served in a variety of civic posts, including "High Bailiff," the municipality's equivalent of mayor. In 1557, he married Robert Arden's youngest daughter, Mary. Mary and John had four sons – William was the oldest – and four daughters, of whom only Joan outlived her most celebrated sibling. William was baptized (an event entered in the Stratford parish church records) on April 26, 1564, and it has become customary, without any good factual support, to suppose he was born on April 23, which happens to be the feast day of Saint George, patron saint of England, and is also the date on which he died, in 1616. Shakespeare married Anne Hathaway in 1582, when he was eighteen and she was twenty-six; their first child was born five months later. It has been generally assumed that the marriage was enforced and subsequently unhappy, but these are only assumptions; it has been estimated, for instance, that up to one third of Elizabethan brides were pregnant when they married. Anne and William Shakespeare had three children: Susanna, who married a prominent local physician, John Hall; and the twins Hamnet, who died young in 1596, and Judith, who married Thomas Quiney – apparently a rather shady individual. The name Hamnet was unusual but not unique: he and his twin sister were named for their godparents, Shakespeare's neighbors Hamnet and Judith Sadler. Shakespeare's father died in 1601 (the year of *Hamlet*), and Mary Arden Shakespeare died in 1608 (the year of *Coriolanus*). William Shakespeare's last surviving direct descendant was his granddaughter Elizabeth Hall, who died in 1670.

Between the birth of the twins in 1585 and a clear reference to Shakespeare as a practicing London dramatist in Robert Greene's sensationalizing, satiric pamphlet, *Greene's Groatsworth of Wit* (1592), there is no record of where William Shakespeare was or what he was doing. These seven so-called lost years have been imaginatively filled by scholars and other students of Shakespeare: some think he traveled to Italy, or fought in the Low Countries, or studied law or medicine, or worked as an apprentice actor/writer, and so on to even more fanciful possibilities. Whatever the biographical facts for those "lost" years, Greene's nasty remarks in 1592 testify to professional envy and to the fact that Shakespeare already had a successful career in London. Speaking to his fellow playwrights, Greene warns both generally and specifically:

> . . . trust them [actors] not: for there is an upstart crow, beautified with our feathers, that with his tiger's heart wrapped in a player's hide supposes he is as well able to bombast out a blank verse as the best of you; and being an absolute Johannes Factotum, is in his own conceit the only Shake-scene in a country.

The passage mimics a line from *3 Henry VI* (hence the play must have been performed before Greene wrote) and seems to say that "Shake-scene" is both actor and play-wright, a jack-of-all-trades. That same year, Henry Chettle protested Greene's remarks in *Kind-Heart's Dream,* and each of the next two years saw the publication of poems – *Venus and Adonis* and *The Rape of Lucrece,* respectively – publicly ascribed to (and dedicated by) Shakespeare. Early in 1595 he was named as one of the senior members of a prominent acting company, the Lord Chamberlain's Men, when they received payment for court performances during the 1594 Christmas season.

Clearly, Shakespeare had achieved both success and reputation in London. In 1596, upon Shakespeare's application, the College of Arms granted his father the now-familiar coat of arms he had taken the first steps to obtain almost twenty years before, and in 1598, John's son – now permitted to call himself "gentleman" – took a 10 percent share in the new Globe playhouse. In 1597, he bought a substantial bourgeois house, called New Place, in Stratford – the garden remains, but Shakespeare's house, several times rebuilt, was torn down in 1759 – and over the next few years Shakespeare spent large sums buying land and making other investments in the town and its environs. Though he worked in London, his family remained in Stratford, and he seems always to have considered Stratford the home he would eventually return to. Something approaching a disinterested appreciation of Shakespeare's popular and professional status appears in Francis Meres's *Palladis Tamia* (1598), a not especially imaginative and perhaps therefore persuasive record of literary reputations. Reviewing contemporary English writers, Meres lists the titles of many of Shakespeare's plays, including one not now known, *Love's Labor's Won,* and praises his "mellifluous & hony-tongued" "sugred Sonnets," which were then circulating in manuscript (they were first collected in 1609). Meres describes Shakespeare as "one of the best" English playwrights of both comedy and tragedy. In *Remains . . . Concerning Britain* (1605),

William Camden – a more authoritative source than the imitative Meres – calls Shakespeare one of the "most pregnant witts of these our times" and joins him with such writers as Chapman, Daniel, Jonson, Marston, and Spenser. During the first decades of the seventeenth century, publishers began to attribute numerous play quartos, including some non-Shakespearean ones, to Shakespeare, either by name or initials, and we may assume that they deemed Shakespeare's name and supposed authorship, true or false, commercially attractive.

For the next ten years or so, various records show Shakespeare's dual career as playwright and man of the theater in London, and as an important local figure in Stratford. In 1608-9 his acting company – designated the "King's Men" soon after King James had succeeded Queen Elizabeth in 1603 – rented, refurbished, and opened a small interior playing space, the Blackfriars theater, in London, and Shakespeare was once again listed as a substantial sharer in the group of proprietors of the playhouse. By May 11, 1612, however, he describes himself as a Stratford resident in a London lawsuit – an indication that he had withdrawn from day-to-day professional activity and returned to the town where he had always had his main financial interests. When Shakespeare bought a substantial residential building in London, the Blackfriars Gatehouse, close to the theater of the same name, on March 10, 1613, he is recorded as William Shakespeare "of Stratford upon Avon in the county of Warwick, gentleman," and he named several London residents as the building's trustees. Still, he continued to participate in theatrical activity: when the new Earl of Rutland needed an allegorical design to bear as a shield, or *impresa,* at the celebration of King James's Accession Day, March 24, 1613, the earl's accountant recorded a payment of 44 shillings to Shakespeare for the device with its motto.

For the last few years of his life, Shakespeare evidently

concentrated his activities in the town of his birth. Most of the final records concern business transactions in Stratford, ending with the notation of his death on April 23, 1616, and burial in Holy Trinity Church, Stratford-upon-Avon.

THE QUESTION OF AUTHORSHIP

The history of ascribing Shakespeare's plays (the poems do not come up so often) to someone else began, as it continues, peculiarly. The earliest published claim that someone else wrote Shakespeare's plays appeared in an 1856 article by Delia Bacon in the American journal *Putnam's Monthly* – although an Englishman, Thomas Wilmot, had shared his doubts in private (even secretive) conversations with friends near the end of the eighteenth century. Bacon's was a sad personal history that ended in madness and poverty, but the year after her article, she published, with great difficulty and the bemused assistance of Nathaniel Hawthorne (then United States Consul in Liverpool, England), her *Philosophy of the Plays of Shakspere Unfolded*. This huge, ornately written, confusing farrago is almost unreadable; sometimes its intents, to say nothing of its arguments, disappear entirely beneath near-raving, ecstatic writing. Tumbled in with much supposed "philosophy" appear the claims that Francis Bacon (from whom Delia Bacon eventually claimed descent), Walter Ralegh, and several other contemporaries of Shakespeare's had written the plays. The book had little impact except as a ridiculed curiosity.

Once proposed, however, the issue gained momentum among people whose conviction was the greater in proportion to their ignorance of sixteenth- and seventeenth-century English literature, history, and society. Another American amateur, Catherine P. Ashmead Windle, made the next influential contribution to the cause when she published *Report to the British Museum* (1882), wherein she promised to open "the Cipher of Francis Bacon," though what she mostly offers, in the words of S. Schoenbaum, is "demented allegorizing." An entire new cottage industry grew from Windle's suggestion that the texts contain hidden, cryptographically discoverable ciphers – "clues" – to their authorship; and today there are not only books devoted to the putative ciphers, but also pamphlets, journals, and newsletters.

Although Baconians have led the pack of those seeking a substitute Shakespeare, in *"Shakespeare" Identified* (1920), J. Thomas Looney became the first published "Oxfordian" when he proposed Edward de Vere, seventeenth earl of Oxford, as the secret author of Shakespeare's plays. Also for Oxford and his "authorship" there are today dedicated societies, articles, journals, and books. Less popular candidates – Queen Elizabeth and Christopher Marlowe among them – have had adherents, but the movement seems to have divided into two main contending factions, Baconian and Oxfordian. (For further details on all the candidates for "Shakespeare," see S. Schoenbaum, *Shakespeare's Lives,* 2nd ed., 1991.)

The Baconians, the Oxfordians, and supporters of other candidates have one trait in common – they are snobs. Every pro-Bacon or pro-Oxford tract sooner or later claims that the historical William Shakespeare of Stratford-upon-Avon could not have written the plays because he could not have had the training, the university education, the experience, and indeed the imagination or background their author supposedly possessed. Only a learned genius like Bacon or an aristocrat like Oxford could have written such fine plays. (As it happens, lucky male children of the middle class had access to better education than most aristocrats in Elizabethan England – and Oxford was not particularly well educated.) Shakespeare received in the Stratford grammar school a formal education that would daunt many college graduates today; and popular rival playwrights such as the very learned Ben Jonson and George Chapman, both of whom also lacked university training, achieved great artistic success, without being taken as Bacon or Oxford.

Besides snobbery, one other quality characterizes the authorship controversy: lack of evidence. A great deal of testimony from Shakespeare's time shows that Shakespeare wrote Shakespeare's plays and that his contemporaries recognized them as distinctive and distinctly superior. (Some of that contemporary evidence is collected in E. K. Chambers, *William Shakespeare: A Study of Facts and Problems*, 2 vols., 1930.) Since that testimony comes from Shakespeare's enemies and theatrical competitors as well as from his co-workers and from the Elizabethan equivalent of literary journalists, it seems unlikely that, if any of these sources had known he was a fraud, they would have failed to record that fact.

Books About Shakespeare's Theater

Useful scholarly studies of theatrical life in Shakespeare's day include: G. E. Bentley, *The Jacobean and Caroline Stage*, 7 vols. (1941–68), and the same author's *The Professions of Dramatist and Player in Shakespeare's Time, 1590-1642* (1986); E. K. Chambers, *The Elizabethan Stage*, 4 vols. (1923); R. A. Foakes, *Illustrations of the English Stage, 1580-1642* (1985); Andrew Gurr, *The Shakespearean Stage*, 3rd ed. (1992), and the same author's *Play-going in Shakespeare's London*, 2nd ed. (1996); Edwin Nungezer, *A Dictionary of Actors* (1929); Carol Chillington Rutter, ed., *Documents of the Rose Playhouse* (1984).

Books About Shakespeare's Life

The following books provide scholarly, documented accounts of Shakespeare's life: G. E. Bentley, *Shakespeare: A Biographical Handbook* (1961); E. K. Chambers, *William Shakespeare: A Study of Facts and Problems*, 2 vols. (1930); S. Schoenbaum, *William Shakespeare: A Compact*

Documentary Life (1977); and *Shakespeare's Lives,* 2nd ed. (1991), by the same author. Many scholarly editions of Shakespeare's complete works print brief compilations of essential dates and events. References to Shakespeare's works up to 1700 are collected in C. M. Ingleby et al., *The Shakespeare Allusion-Book,* rev. ed., 2 vols. (1932).

The Texts of Shakespeare

As FAR AS WE KNOW, only one manuscript conceivably in
Shakespeare's own hand may (and even this is much dis-
puted) exist: a few pages of a play called *Sir Thomas More,*
which apparently was never performed. What we do have,
as later readers, performers, scholars, students, are printed
texts. The earliest of these survive in two forms: quartos
and folios. Quartos (from the Latin for "four") are small
books, printed on sheets of paper that were then folded in
fours, to make eight double-sided pages. When these were
bound together, the result was a squarish, eminently
portable volume that sold for the relatively small sum of
sixpence (translating in modern terms to about $5.00). In
folios, on the other hand, the sheets are folded only once,
in half, producing large, impressive volumes taller than
they are wide. This was the format for important works of
philosophy, science, theology, and literature (the major
precedent for a folio Shakespeare was Ben Jonson's *Works,*
1616). The decision to print the works of a popular playwright in folio is an indication of how far up on the social
scale the theatrical profession had come during Shakespeare's lifetime. The Shakespeare folio was an expensive
book, selling for between fifteen and eighteen shillings,
depending on the binding (in modern terms, from about
$150 to $180). Twenty Shakespeare plays of the thirty-
seven that survive first appeared in quarto, seventeen of
which appeared during Shakespeare's lifetime; the rest of
the plays are found only in folio.

The First Folio was published in 1623, seven years after
Shakespeare's death, and was authorized by his fellow actors, the co-owners of the King's Men. This publication

was certainly a mark of the company's enormous respect for Shakespeare; but it was also a way of turning the old plays, most of which were no longer current in the playhouse, into ready money (the folio includes only Shakespeare's plays, not his sonnets or other nondramatic verse). Whatever the motives behind the publication of the folio, the texts it preserves constitute the basis for almost all later editions of the playwright's works. The texts, however, differ from those of the earlier quartos, sometimes in minor respects but often significantly – most strikingly in the two texts of *King Lear,* but also in important ways in *Hamlet, Othello,* and *Troilus and Cressida.* (The variants are recorded in the textual notes to each play in the new Pelican series.) The differences in these texts represent, in a sense, the essence of theater: the texts of plays were initially not intended for publication. They were scripts, designed for the actors to perform – the principal life of the play at this period was in performance. And it follows that in Shakespeare's theater the playwright typically had no say either in how his play was performed or in the disposition of his text – he was an employee of the company. The authoritative figures in the theatrical enterprise were the shareholders in the company, who were for the most part the major actors. They decided what plays were to be done; they hired the playwright and often gave him an outline of the play they wanted him to write. Often, too, the play was a collaboration: the company would retain a group of writers, and parcel out the scenes among them. The resulting script was then the property of the company, and the actors would revise it as they saw fit during the course of putting it on stage. The resulting text belonged to the company. The playwright had no rights in it once he had been paid. (This system survives largely intact in the movie industry, and most of the playwrights of Shakespeare's time were as anonymous as most screenwriters are today.) The script could also, of course, continue to change as the tastes of audiences and the requirements of the actors changed. Many – perhaps most – plays were revised when they were reintroduced after any substantial absence from the repertory, or when they were performed by a company different from the one that originally commissioned the play.

Shakespeare was an exceptional figure in this world because he was not only a shareholder and actor in his company, but also its leading playwright – he was literally his own boss. He had, moreover, little interest in the publication of his plays, and even those that appeared during his lifetime with the authorization of the company show no signs of any editorial concern on the part of the author. Theater was, for Shakespeare, a fluid and supremely responsive medium – the very opposite of the great classic canonical text that has embodied his works since 1623.

The very fluidity of the original texts, however, has meant that Shakespeare has always had to be edited. Here is an example of how problematic the editorial project inevitably is, a passage from the most famous speech in *Romeo and Juliet*, Juliet's balcony soliloquy beginning "O Romeo, Romeo, wherefore art thou Romeo?" Since the eighteenth century, the standard modern text has read,

> What's Montague? It is nor hand, nor foot,
> Nor arm, nor face, nor any other part
> Belonging to a man. O be some other name!
> What's in a name? That which we call a rose
> By any other name would smell as sweet.
>
> (II.2.40-44)

Editors have three early texts of this play to work from, two quarto texts and the folio. Here is how the First Quarto (1597) reads:

> Whats *Mountague*? It is nor band nor foote,
> Nor arme, nor face, nor any other part.
> Whats in a name? That which we call a Rofe,
> By any other name would fmell as fweet:

Here is the Second Quarto (1599):

> Whats *Mountague*? it is nor hand nor foote,
> Nor arme nor face, ô be fome other name
> Belonging to a man.
> Whats in a name that which we call a rofe,
> By any other word would fmell as fweete,

And here is the First Folio (1623):

> What's *Mountague*? it is nor hand nor foote,
> Nor arme, nor face, O be fome other name
> Belonging to a man.
> What? in a names that which we call a Rofe,
> By any other word would fmell as fweete,

There is in fact no early text that reads as our modern text does – and this is the most famous speech in the play. Instead, we have three quite different texts, all of which are clearly some version of the same speech, but none of which seems to us a final or satisfactory version. The transcendently beautiful passage in modern editions is an editorial invention: editors have succeeded in conflating and revising the three versions into something we recognize as great poetry. Is this what Shakespeare "really" wrote? Who can say? What we can say is that Shakespeare always had performance, not a book, in mind.

Books About the Shakespeare Texts

The standard study of the printing history of the First Folio is W. W. Greg, *The Shakespeare First Folio* (1955). J. K. Walton, *The Quarto Copy for the First Folio of Shakespeare* (1971), is a useful survey of the relation of the quartos to the folio. The second edition of Charlton Hinman's *Norton Facsimile* of the First Folio (1996), with a new introduction by Peter Blayney, is indispensable. Stanley Wells, Gary Taylor, John Jowett, and William Montgomery, *William Shakespeare: A Textual Companion,* keyed to the Oxford text, gives a comprehensive survey of the editorial situation for all the plays and poems.

THE GENERAL EDITORS

Introduction

In 1611 Dr. Simon Forman, physician and astrologer, went to see *Cymbeline*. There are so few accounts of a Shakespeare play being performed in Shakespeare's lifetime that it is worth giving Forman's account in full:

Remember also the story of Cymbeline, King of England in Lucius' time. How Lucius came from Octavius Caesar for tribute and, being denied, after sent Lucius with a great army of soldiers who landed at Milford Haven and after were vanquished by Cymbeline and Lucius taken prisoner. And all by means of three outlaws of the which two of them were the sons of Cymbeline, stolen from him when they were but two years old by an old man whom Cymbeline banished and he kept them as his own sons twenty years with him in a cave. And how one of them slew Cloten that was the queen's son, going to Milford Haven to seek the love of Innogen, the king's daughter whom he had banished also for loving his daughter. And how the Italian that came from her love conveyed himself into a chest and said it was a chest of plate sent from her love and others to be presented to the King. And in the deepest of the night, she being asleep, he opened the chest and came forth of it. And viewed her in her bed and the marks of her body and took away her bracelet and after accused her of adultery to her love, etc. And in the end how he came with the Romans into England and was taken prisoner and after revealed to Innogen, who had turned herself into man's apparel and fled to meet her love at Milford Haven and chanced to fall on the cave in the woods where her two brothers were. And how by eating a sleeping dram they thought she had been dead and laid her in the woods and the body of Cloten by her in her love's apparel that he left behind him and how she was found by Lucius, etc.

As in the other notes on plays he saw that year, Forman makes a number of mistakes about details of the plot, at least in the form in which the play was printed in the First Folio, published in 1623: Cymbeline, for instance, did not banish the "old man," Belarius, and it was Posthumus, not Cloten, whom Cymbeline banished. But Forman also seems to have found it peculiarly difficult to recount the plot of *Cymbeline* in anything approaching the right sequential order. He would not be the last, for the multiple actions of the play can easily confuse.

For some the play is simply a failure. Dr. Johnson, in his edition (1765), found the play's complex dramaturgy too much:

> To remark the folly of the fiction, the absurdity of the conduct, the confusion of the names and manners of different times and the impossibility of the events in any system of life, were to waste criticism upon unresisting imbecility, upon faults too evident for detection and too gross for aggravation.

Modern critics have often resorted to the word "experimental" to describe the remarkable assemblage of different materials that Shakespeare sought – in the view of many, unsuccessfully – to combine into a single play. More than one critic has turned to Polonius's celebration of the skills of the acting company visiting Elsinore and defined *Cymbeline*, with varying degrees of irony, as a "tragical-comical-historical-pastoral." The order in which Shakespeare wrote his last unaided plays is far from clear, and the traditional ordering, in which *Cymbeline* was followed by *The Winter's Tale* and *The Tempest,* is no more than a convention that serves, too neatly, to explain away *Cymbeline* as Shakespeare's attempt at a new kind of drama. But such a sequence, even apart from its ignoring both the significance of *Pericles* and the difficulties in establishing the date of *Cymbeline* more firmly than that it must have been written before Forman saw it, undervalues the complexity of Shakespeare's enormously ambitious project in *Cymbeline* and his accomplishment of so much of it. It is a play that theater audiences have enjoyed and admired far more than critics, and this theatrical success argues that *Cymbeline* should be seen as an experiment worthy of a more profound admiration than the use of Polonius's label might suggest. Nonetheless, Polonius's categories of dramatic genre provide a pattern for considering the play, though I shall, remembering Forman's difficulties with the sequence of plots, reorder Polonius's sequence.

Forman was clearly struck by the battle between Romans and Britons and its turning point when, in Posthumus's exhilarating account, Belarius, Guiderius, and Arviragus turn the chaotic retreat of Cymbeline's army into a great victory. As the lord comments, "This was strange chance: / A narrow lane, an old man, and two boys" (V.3.51-52). Shakespeare found this element of his plot in Holinshed's *Chronicles,* the work from which he drew other fragments of his narrative and the source, as so often, for his historical drama. The story does not appear anywhere near Holinshed's account of Cymbeline; instead, Shakespeare adapted it from an account in Holinshed's *Description and History of Scotland* of an event in a battle between the Scots and the Danes, perhaps a passage he had read when writing *Macbeth.* But the story of Hay and his two sons — which has no trace of the narrative of stolen babies in it — had a particular topical relevance: the Hay of Holinshed's tale was an ancestor of Lord Hay, a close friend of King

James, created a Knight of the Bath in 1610 at the installation of the Prince of Wales.

Perhaps very few members of the audience at the early performances of *Cymbeline* would have picked up the reference – Forman does not appear to have noticed it – but, taken with so many other details in the play, it makes the play emphatically topical, a deliberate exploration of and celebration by Shakespeare of King James's political plans. As with the narrow lane, Shakespeare did not find anywhere in or near the *Chronicles'* accounts of Cymbeline any reason to direct Imogen's wanderings toward Milford Haven, a place-name so often spoken in the play. Shakespeare had referred to Milford once in an earlier play, when Richard III is told that "the Earl of Richmond / Is with a mighty power landed at Milford" (*Richard III,* IV.4.532–33). Richmond would be crowned as Henry VII, and hence Milford was the point in the country where the invasion that inaugurated the Tudor dynasty started. It is in *Cymbeline* the only place in Britain to be mentioned apart from Lud's town. Just as the name of the capital, London, is archaized into revealing the name of its mythic founder – King Lud, who was Cymbeline's grandfather – so the play draws its strands together at the place that founded the Tudors and, by extension, defined James's right to the British throne, since Henry VII was James's great-grandfather.

Holinshed had to admit that he could find very little in his sources about the reign of Cymbeline beyond the fact that he was brought up in Rome:

> Little other mention is made of his doings, except that during his reign the Saviour of the world, our Lord Jesus Christ, the only Son of God, was born of a virgin, about the 23rd year of the reign of this Cymbeline.

Where we might imagine Cymbeline as ruler at some vaguely mythic point in British history, Shakespeare – and probably many in his audience – would have known him as king at a precise and potent moment of historical beginning, the moment of Christ's birth. The play's final image of peace is on the surface an indication of a final resolution of the war between Rome and Britain, but it also suggests the larger peace of Christ. In *Antony and Cleopatra* Octavius, who would become the Emperor Augustus, ruler of Rome at the time of Cymbeline, announces that "The time of universal peace is near" (IV.6.5). Pax Romana, the Roman-ruled peace across the massive expanse of the Roman empire, is an earthly counterpart to the Christian peace. The peace at the end of *Cymbeline* is not a weak submission to the rule of Rome but an acceptance by the victor of the obligation of paying tribute to the defeated. Harmoniously and collaboratively, Rome and Britain envision a future of peace. For Holinshed it was Guiderius, not Cymbeline, who refused to pay tribute to Rome but, more potently for Shakespeare's audience, it was Henry VIII who refused to pay "Peter's Pence" to the Roman Catholic Church from 1534. In the new realm envisaged at the end of *Cymbeline* there could be a different accommodation between nation-states.

But the play's two defined historical periods, the time of the birth of Christ and the time of the birth of the Tudor dynasty, hint at other beginnings. There has been a long dispute over the name Shakespeare gave his heroine in *Cymbeline*. The First Folio consistently prints it as "Imogen" – and I have kept to that form in this edition – but Shakespeare, in a stage direction in *Much Ado About Nothing*, has a character named "Innogen," and that is the name Forman recorded when he saw *Cymbeline*. "Innogen" is also the name that Holinshed noted as the wife of Brut, according to Holinshed a descendant of Aeneas and the founder of Britain – and Shakespeare may well have chosen the name of Imogen's husband, Posthumus, to echo the name of Brut's grandfather in Holinshed. As Imogen or Innogen the name connects to the origins of Britain and to its Trojan founders.

Throughout his last plays, Shakespeare was concerned with the problem of inheritance and succession: in *The Winter's Tale,* the death of Mamillius and the disappearance of Perdita will, as the oracle warns, leave the King of Sicilia living without an heir; the marriage of Ferdinand and Miranda in *The Tempest* will unite Milan and Naples in a new dynasty. In *Cymbeline,* the opening political situation concerns a proposed marriage between a commoner – albeit one brought up as Cymbeline's personal servant – and the apparent sole surviving heir to Cymbeline's kingdom, for Imogen is repeatedly referred to by her title as "princess" (e.g., at I.1.16). Helena Faucit, the nineteenth-century actress, suggested that the play should be retitled *Imogen, Princess of Britain,* in honor of the character her audiences saw as central to the play. At the end of the play the king's new family – his unnamed queen and her son Cloten – is dead, and his lost children found. The kingdom, which through much of the play has lacked any heir, now has three, and the problems posed by Imogen's marriage out of her class have diminished. Only the recovery of the missing male heirs can enable the princess's marriage to a commoner no longer to pose such a strong threat to the succession.

Though Forman headed his notes "Of Cymbeline, King of England," the country where the action of *Cymbeline* takes place is emphatically Britain, not England. "England" is a word entirely absent from *Cymbeline* while, of Shakespeare's sixty-five uses of "Britain" and its cognates, all but eighteen appear in this play. The word suggests both a historic past and a new and larger concept of nation, as James had sought to unite two countries, England and Scotland, into a new one, to be known as "Great Britain," a place where Scots born after James's accession in 1603 were called Post Nati, a label buried in the name of *Cymbeline*'s "hero," Posthumus Leonatus. The Renaissance doctrine of the westward translation of empire, the belief that the seat of the successive empires of the known world moved west from Troy to Rome, would now find its third home in James's kingdom, ruled by a monarch who recurrently modeled himself on Augustus. The soothsayer, before the climactic battle, interpreted his vision of the flight of the Roman eagle from the south to the west as an omen of Roman victory. In the aftermath of defeat and, more significantly, of the multiple revelations of the last scene, the vision demands to be read afresh as a manifestation of the union of Rome and Britain, of Augustus and Cymbeline, whose radiance "shines here in the west" (V.5.478) in the united Britain that James envisioned.

Cymbeline's ancient Britain merges with a modern Europe where Romans have become Italians like Iachimo and Philario and where the exiled Posthumus meets Philario's friends, who are identified in I.4 only by their nationality: a Frenchman, a Dutchman, and a Spaniard. "Britain" in the play is not an absolute but a state that needs to take its place in a context defined by the other nations of Europe. As Imogen is forced to recognize, there is more to the world than can be found in Britain:

> Hath Britain all the sun that shines? Day, night,
> Are they not but in Britain? I' th' world's volume
> Our Britain seems as of it, but not in't;
> In a great pool a swan's nest. Prithee think
> There's livers out of Britain.
>
> (III.4.137–41)

By the end of the play, in the diplomatic solution of the international politics, Britain is firmly located in the "world's volume," part of the new future for European history.

The play's two time frames coexist so that Iachimo, the epitome of contemporary Italianate villainy (in contrast to the decent Roman virtues of Lucius), the heir in more

than name to *Othello*'s Iago, fights in the army of the
Roman emperor, Augustus. *Cymbeline* is the last play in
the First Folio volume, placed among the tragedies and
perhaps only for that reason called "The Tragedy of Cymbeline." Yet much of its action teeters on the brink of
tragedy. Shakespeare's sources for the wager story were
primarily a tale in Boccaccio's *Decameron* (Second Day,
Ninth Tale) and a German version translated as *Frederick
of Jennen* (first published in English in 1518). In such
narratives there is no question of the rule of kingdoms.
Bourgeois accounts of suspicion and duplicity, they end
happily. But the false accusation of unchastity and adultery could easily end in tragedy, as it had in Shakespeare's
Lucrece (to whose rapist, Tarquin, Iachimo compares himself at II.2.12–14) or *Othello*, and as the accusation of
Hero in *Much Ado About Nothing* or Hermione in *The
Winter's Tale* so nearly did. The completed span of *Cymbeline* denies tragedy but sustainedly engages with tragedy
as a possibility.

Unlike the grander diabolism of Iago, Iachimo's motives are a clearer combination of greed and arrogance.
Iachimo's distrust of Posthumus's reputation in the conversation in I.4 that precedes Posthumus's appearance at
Philario's is key. Iachimo values Posthumus's "marrying
his king's daughter" by Imogen's worth, not her husband's. It will be the revelation of Imogen's worth, her
value, that proves to necessitate Iachimo's trunk trick,
since his belying Posthumus's behavior, his offer of a
revaluation of his worth, has no effect. Iachimo's "false report" (I.6.173) to Imogen of Posthumus is ineffective because Iachimo's proposal that Imogen take revenge by
having sex with Iachimo is immediately read by Imogen
as proving the untruth of his account of her husband:

> If thou wert honorable,
> Thou wouldst have told this tale for virtue, not
> For such an end thou seek'st, as base as strange.

Thou wrong'st a gentleman who is as far
From thy report as thou from honor . . .
                    (I.6.142-46)

Iachimo's language of value has quickly induced in
Posthumus a shift from valuing Imogen – and his ring,
the symbol of that love and betrothal – as "More than the
world enjoys" (I.4.76) to prizing or pricing her chastity at
precisely ten thousand ducats. As in that other play of
ducats and rings, *The Merchant of Venice,* the man's will-
ingness to part with the token of his marriage makes of
the ring a bond between men, not between husband and
wife. But in *Cymbeline* the ring more quickly takes on its
common meaning of representing the female genitalia,
the sexuality that a man cannot control. Imogen, who
elsewhere in the play can be identified as Britain (as in her
own comment to Iachimo, "My lord, I fear, / Has forgot
Britain" I.6.112-13), is now equivalent to the diamond
ring. From a romance language of the identification of the
loved woman as beyond value, Posthumus becomes part
of a wager of mercantile exchange.

When Cloten encourages his musicians to serenade
Imogen with a dawn song in II.3, the result is one of
Shakespeare's most beautiful lyrics, "Hark, hark, the lark
at heaven's gate sings," but the song is framed by Cloten's
sleazy language of sexual implication in which the music
penetrating her ear might enable Cloten's penis to penetrate her body. Cloten's version of sex with Imogen comes
the morning after Iachimo, in the trunk, has penetrated
her chamber. The room and its occupant merge; the
chamber is Imogen's body. As she went to sleep in II.2,
Imogen was reading the tale of Tereus's rape and mutila-
tion of Philomela, perhaps where Shakespeare himself had
read it, in Book 6 of Ovid's *Metamorphoses.* In *Titus Andronicus,* the raped and mutilated Lavinia had used her
nephew's copy of Ovid's narration of this brutal act to explain to her father what had happened to her. In *Cymbe-*

line the myth serves as a hint of what might physically have occurred. But if Imogen is not raped in the conventional meaning of the word, the penetration of her room and the visual exploration of her sleeping body constitute a rape of another and devastating kind. There are few moments in Shakespeare in which the female body is quite so sensuously itemized and sexually available. The mole "on" – or in Iachimo's retelling at II.4.134, "under" – her left breast is a "secret," a mark of identification in itself sufficient to "force [Posthumus] think I have picked the lock and ta'en / The treasure of her honor" (II.2.41–42). It is no surprise that Forman recorded how Iachimo "viewed her in her bed and the marks of her body." Visual knowledge of her body is enough to represent to her husband sexual knowledge of it.

This belief generates in Posthumus a speech – the soliloquy making up the whole of II.5 – that constitutes the most violent expression of misogyny in all Shakespeare: "For there's no motion / That tends to vice in man but I affirm / It is the woman's part." In its tormented loathing of women, this language is an expression of agony the equal of any moment in Shakespearean tragedy. Neither the fact that it is the product of his gullibility, parallel to Othello's, nor the vicious untruth of these ravings diminishes its threatening power. Nor does the fact that the emotion will be changed by the end of the play, for in *Cymbeline* the characters' most extreme expressions of the emotions of tragedy are often circumscribed by the truth of event and the transformability of the action.

Later the play, in IV.2, sharply juxtaposes two laments, neither of which is justified, for Guiderius and Arviragus's spoken song lamenting over the corpse of Imogen is denied by the fact that she is not dead, and Imogen's agonized lament over the headless corpse is denied by the fact that the body is Cloten's, not Posthumus's. But by this point the play has moved from court to country, from a world of politics and intrigue to a context for pastoral. Where to put the interval is often a problem for directors of modern productions of Shakespeare plays, but at the moment when Belarius and his two "sons" enter from their cave at the beginning of III.3, the drama takes on a new guise and a new genre.

As Shakespeare and his younger contemporaries Francis Beaumont and John Fletcher began to explore the new possibilities in a drama of pastoral romance, they drew on a range of sources, from prose works like Sir Philip Sidney's *Arcadia* or epic poems like Spenser's *Faerie Queene* or Tasso's *Jerusalem Delivered* (translated by Edward Fairfax in 1600) to drama long out of fashion. For *Cymbeline* Shakespeare probably used anonymous plays like *Mucedorus* (first performed c. 1590 but revived and revised in 1610) and *Sir Clyomon and Sir Clamydes* (first performed in the 1570s). There are more direct echoes of another anonymous play, *The Rare Triumphs of Love and Fortune* (performed 1582, published 1589). The vision of Jupiter in *Cymbeline* has roots in the spectacle of court masque, transferred to the public theaters in new ways – Jupiter's entrance sitting on an eagle may have been the first time in a public play in which a character flew on in this fashion – but the battle between the gods in *Rare Triumphs* may lie behind Jupiter's statement of divine intervention: "Whom best I love I cross; to make my gift, / The more delayed, delighted" (V.4.101-2).

But the materials of romance are conventional. Any audience would know that when a gentleman in the first scene announces that Cymbeline's sons were stolen "and to this hour no guess in knowledge / Which way they went" (I.1.60-61), the missing heirs are bound to appear sooner or later. Whatever the diffuseness of plotting that such tales involve, the audience must be sure that the disparate threads and wandering characters will eventually converge. The landscape in which the convergence takes place is a wild vision of Wales. In this inhospitable place of woods and cave, where hunting is no longer a royal pastime but a necessity for finding food, the all-male family of Belarius, Guiderius, and Arviragus are renamed into Morgan, Polydore, and Cadwal, names that suggest a less Latinate, native tradition. There are no women in this world: Euriphile, the boys' "mother," is dead, and Imogen can exist here only by following Pisanio's suggestion, "You must forget to be a woman" (III.4.155). Indeed, as the play draws toward its end, women are turned into thin, though "tender," air, as the improbable etymology of the Latin word "mulier" from "mollis aer" explains the enigmatic reference in the book Posthumus finds after the appearance of Jupiter.

It is only by discovering and incorporating the kinds of natural response appropriate to living in this harsh pastoral – like Guiderius's response to the court insults of Cloten, a response untrammeled by notions of status – that the comic solution can be envisaged and the last of Polonius's genres encompassed. But the ending of *Cymbeline* has been a particular trial for critics. George Bernard Shaw, for all his admiration for the play, was so sure that it "goes to pieces in the last act" that he wrote a new final act, performed in London in 1937. Initially convinced that Act V was "a cobbled-up *pasticcio* by other hands," Shaw came to realize that it "is genuine Shakespear [*sic*] to the last full stop" and that the vision was not "scraps of quite ridiculous doggerel" but "a versified masque, in Shakespear's careless woodnotes wild." For Shaw, indeed, the vision, "with the very Shakespearean feature of a comic jailor which precedes it," was "just the thing to save the last act," for "without it the act is a tedious string of unsurprising *dénouements* sugared with insincere sentimentality after a ludicrous stage battle."

Certainly the last act does not read well, and critics unresponsive to the theater have assumed that it therefore could not play well. Shaw's *Cymbeline Refinished* reads much more easily in its reining back on the sheer welter of revelations. But in good productions the slow unfolding of the mysteries of action, the careful untangling of the drama's confusions, is a remarkable combination of two forms of comedy. For while the audience laughs at the comedy of improbable twists and turns, it is also moved by the play's drive to a comedic resolution. *Cymbeline*'s ending is inclusive in many senses as the characters are brought back together and as the vision has brought onto the stage another complete, though dead, family, Posthumus's parents and two brothers mirroring Imogen's. But there can be no place in this new interweaving for Cymbeline's substitute family, his stepson Cloten and the wicked stepmother queen – straight out of fairy tales like *Snow White* – whose destructive ambitions for her son and advocacy of war as the correct mode of international diplomacy have been superseded. The reassembling of the characters and the reforming of the families and relationships that they define, from husband and wife through father and children to king and heirs, are also an amalgamation of dramatic genres.

Is it striking that Forman failed to mention the vision of Jupiter? Some have argued that it was a late addition to the play, not present in the version Forman saw. But perhaps he had simply run out of interest in things that he needed to "remember." The end of *Cymbeline* takes place under the aegis of Jupiter in a context in which the most important action is a religious celebration – "Laud we the gods," as Cymbeline states at the opening of the final speech (V.5.478). But the sheer theatricality of the vision also leads to the careful laying bare of the mechanics of ending in the expanse of the final scene. Shakespeare is not afraid to make the plot deliberately creak at the end of comedy: in *The Merchant of Venice* Portia brings Antonio news of his ships' safe return, telling him – and the audience – "You shall not know by what strange accident / I chancèd on this letter"; Duke Frederick and his army in *As You Like It* are stopped offstage on the fringes of the

Forest of Arden by a chance encounter with "an old religious man." But in *Cymbeline* Shakespeare makes matters far less improbable; once the audience overcomes the difficulty of accepting that everyone might reasonably turn up near Milford Haven, drawn there by the magnet of the story, the ending of the drama plays out, fully and probably, the consequences of this gathering. It is theatricality of a different kind from the solutions to earlier plays, a pleasure in the joys of ending narratives and of storytelling itself. In the magnificent transfer of the devices of narrative into a new – and often leisurely – dramatic form, Shakespeare accomplished something that was more complex than Simon Forman could record.

PETER HOLLAND
The Shakespeare Institute,
The University of Birmingham

Note on the Text

CYMBELINE WAS FIRST published in the First Folio of
1623. Textual scholars are divided in their opinions about
the nature of the copy used by the printers: it was probably a transcript by a professional scribe, perhaps Ralph
Crane, though it is unclear whether the scribe worked
from a theater promptbook. In any case, the folio text is a
reasonably good one, and it has been followed closely in
the present edition. The act-scene division provided here
for reference is that of the Globe text, which departs from
the division of the folio at three points (indicated below):
I.1 combining folio I.1 and 2; II.4 and 5 dividing folio II.4;
and III.6 combining folio III.6 and 7. Departures from the
folio text, except for relincations, normalization of speech
prefixes, modernization of spelling and punctuation, and
correction of obvious typographical errors, are listed below.
Adopted readings are given in italics, followed by the folio
(F) readings.

I.1. 4 ff FIRST GENTLEMAN (from here on, F assigns the speeches of the two
Gentlemen simply to "1" and "2"; so also for the two Lords in I.2, II.1,
and II.3, and for the two Captains in V.3) 70 (F begins Scene 2 here)
I.3 9 *this* his
I.4 42 *offend not* offend 68 *Britain* Britanie 70 *not but* not 80 *pur-
chase* purchases 124 *thousand* thousands
I.5 3 s.d. *Exeunt* Exit
I.6 7 *desire* desires 24 *truest* trust 28 *takes* take 108 *by-peeping* by
peeping 168 *men's* men 169 *descended* defended
II.1 33 *tonight* night 60 *husband, than* Husband. Then 61 *make. The*
make the 64 s.d. *Exit* Exeunt
II.2 49 *bare* beare
II.3 29 *vice* voyce 31 *amend* amed 47 *solicits* solicity 137 *garment*
Garments 154 *you* your
II.4 6 *hopes* hope 24 *mingled* wing-led 34 *through* thorough 36 *tenor*
tenure 37 *PHILARIO* Post. 47 *not* note 57 *you* yon 116 *one of* one
135 *the* her

II.5 16 *German one* Iarmen on   27 *man may name* name
III.1 20 *rocks* Oakes
III.2 67 *score* store   78 *nor* not
III.3 2 *Stoop* Sleepe   23 *robe* Babe   28 *know* knowes   83 *wherein they bow* whereon the Bowe
III.4 79 *afore't* a-foot   90 *make* makes   102 *eyeballs out* eye-balles
III.5 32 *looks* looke   40 *strokes* stroke   53 s.d. *[Exit Messenger.]* (not in F)
   55 s.d. *Exit* (appears after *days* in F)   139 *insultment* insulment
III.6 28 (F begins Scene 7 here)   57 *Whither* Whether
IV.1 13 *imperceiverant* imperseuerant
IV.2 49–51 *He . . . dieter* (F assigns these lines to Arviragus)   50 *sauced* sawc'st   58 *patience* patient   122 *thank* thanks   205 *crare* care   206 *Might* Might'st   224 *ruddock* Raddocke   290 *is* are
IV.4 2 *find we* we finde   17 *the* their
V.1 1 *wished* am wisht
V.3 24 *harts* hearts   42 *stooped* stopt   43 *they* the
V.4 29 s.d. *follow* followes   67 *geck* geeke   81 *look out* looke,/looke out
V.5 65 *heard* heare   208 *got it* got   264 *from* fro   337 *mere* neere   381 *ye* we   389 *brothers* Brother   408 *so* no   471 *this yet* yet this

Cymbeline

[Names of the Actors

CYMBELINE, *King of Britain*
IMOGEN, *daughter to Cymbeline by a former queen*
GUIDERIUS ⎱ *sons to Cymbeline, disguised under*
⎰ *the names of Polydore and Cadwal,*
ARVIRAGUS ⎰ *supposed sons of Morgan*
QUEEN, *wife to Cymbeline*
CLOTEN, *son to the queen by a former husband*
BELARIUS, *a banished lord, disguised under the*
name of Morgan
CORNELIUS, *a physician*
HELEN, *a lady attending on Imogen*
TWO LORDS *of Cymbeline's court attending on*
Cloten
TWO GENTLEMEN *of Cymbeline's court*
TWO BRITISH CAPTAINS
TWO JAILERS

POSTHUMUS LEONATUS, *a gentleman, husband*
to Imogen
PISANIO, *servant to Posthumus*
PHILARIO, *friend to Posthumus* ⎱
IACHIMO, *friend to Philario* ⎰ *Italians*
A FRENCHMAN
A DUTCHMAN
A SPANIARD

CAIUS LUCIUS, *General of the Roman forces*
TWO ROMAN SENATORS
ROMAN TRIBUNES
A ROMAN CAPTAIN
PHILARMONUS, *a soothsayer*

JUPITER
GHOST OF SICILIUS LEONATUS, *father of Posthumus*
GHOST OF MOTHER OF POSTHUMUS
GHOSTS OF BROTHERS OF POSTHUMUS

LORDS *attending on Cymbeline*
LADIES *attending on the queen*
MUSICIANS *attending on Cloten*
MESSENGERS, SOLDIERS, ATTENDANTS

SCENE: *Britain, Rome*]
*

Cymbeline

∾ I.1 *Enter two Gentlemen.*

FIRST GENTLEMAN
   You do not meet a man but frowns. Our bloods   1
   No more obey the heavens than our courtiers
   Still seem as does the king's.   3
SECOND GENTLEMAN   But what's the matter?
FIRST GENTLEMAN
   His daughter, and the heir of's kingdom, whom
   He purposed to his wife's sole son – a widow   5
   That late he married – hath referred herself   6
   Unto a poor but worthy gentleman. She's wedded,
   Her husband banished, she imprisoned. All
   Is outward sorrow, though I think the king
   Be touched at very heart.   10
SECOND GENTLEMAN   None but the king?
FIRST GENTLEMAN
   He that hath lost her too. So is the queen,
   That most desired the match. But not a courtier,
   Although they wear their faces to the bent   13
   Of the king's looks, hath a heart that is not
   Glad at the thing they scowl at.
SECOND GENTLEMAN   And why so?
FIRST GENTLEMAN
   He that hath missed the princess is a thing

I.1 Britain: the palace of King Cymbeline **1** *bloods* moods **3** *seem . . .
king's* adjust their demeanor to the king's mood or expression (cf. ll. 13–14)
5 *purposed to* intended for **6** *referred* given **13** *bent* cast

Too bad for bad report, and he that hath her –
I mean, that married her, alack good man,
And therefore banished – is a creature such
20   As, to seek through the regions of the earth
For one his like, there would be something failing
22   In him that should compare. I do not think
So fair an outward and such stuff within
24   Endows a man but he.
SECOND GENTLEMAN   You speak him far.
FIRST GENTLEMAN
25   I do extend him, sir, within himself,
26   Crush him together rather than unfold
His measure duly.
SECOND GENTLEMAN   What's his name and birth?
FIRST GENTLEMAN
28   I cannot delve him to the root. His father
29   Was called Sicilius, who did join his honor
30   Against the Romans with Cassibelan,
But had his titles by Tenantius, whom
He served with glory and admired success,
33   So gained the sur-addition Leonatus;
And had, besides this gentleman in question,
Two other sons, who in the wars o' th' time
Died with their swords in hand; for which their father,
37   Then old and fond of issue, took such sorrow
That he quit being, and his gentle lady,
39   Big of this gentleman our theme, deceased
40   As he was born. The king he takes the babe

---

22 *him . . . compare* the man picked to be comparable   24 *speak him far* go
far in praise of him   25 *extend . . . himself* expand upon his actual qualities
26–27 *Crush . . . duly* diminish his worth rather than reveal his true stature
28 *delve . . . root* dig to the root of his family tree   29 *did . . . honor* con-
tributed his military fame   30–31 *Cassibelan, Tenantius* British rulers mentioned by Holinshed or other chroniclers: Cassibelan was Cymbeline's
great-uncle ("uncle" at III.1.5); Tenantius was Cymbeline's father, son of
King Lud   33 *sur-addition* added title   37 *fond of issue* loving his children
39 *Big . . . theme* pregnant with Posthumus

To his protection, calls him Posthumus Leonatus,
Breeds him and makes him of his bedchamber,   42
Puts to him all the learnings that his time   43
Could make him the receiver of, which he took
As we do air, fast as 'twas ministered,
And in's spring became a harvest, lived in court –
Which rare it is to do – most praised, most loved,
A sample to the youngest, to th' more mature   48
A glass that feated them, and to the graver   49
A child that guided dotards. To his mistress,   50
For whom he now is banished – her own price   51
Proclaims how she esteemed him and his virtue.
By her election may be truly read   53
What kind of man he is.

SECOND GENTLEMAN   I honor him
Even out of your report. But pray you tell me,
Is she sole child to th' king?

FIRST GENTLEMAN   His only child.
He had two sons – if this be worth your hearing,
Mark it – the eldest of them at three years old,
I' th' swathing clothes the other, from their nursery   59
Were stol'n, and to this hour no guess in knowledge   60
Which way they went.

SECOND GENTLEMAN   How long is this ago?

FIRST GENTLEMAN
Some twenty years.

SECOND GENTLEMAN
That a king's children should be so conveyed,   63
So slackly guarded, and the search so slow
That could not trace them!

---

42 *of his bedchamber* one of his personal servants 43 *time* age 48 *sample*
example 49 *glass . . . them* mirror that reflected them as elegantly as they
would wish to be 50 *guided dotards* provided a model of behavior even for
old dodderers; *To* as for 51 *price* i.e., the price she paid 53 *election* choice
59 *swathing* swaddling 60 *guess in knowledge* conjecture leading to knowledge 63 *conveyed* taken away (i.e., stolen)

FIRST GENTLEMAN   Howsoe'er 'tis strange,
66   Or that the negligence may well be laughed at,
      Yet is it true, sir.
SECOND GENTLEMAN   I do well believe you.
FIRST GENTLEMAN
      We must forbear. Here comes the gentleman,
      The queen, and princess.   *Exeunt.*
          Enter the Queen, Posthumus, and Imogen.
QUEEN
70   No, be assured you shall not find me, daughter,
      After the slander of most stepmothers,
      Evil-eyed unto you. You're my prisoner, but
      Your jailer shall deliver you the keys
74   That lock up your restraint. For you, Posthumus,
      So soon as I can win th' offended king,
76   I will be known your advocate. Marry, yet
      The fire of rage is in him, and 'twere good
78   You leaned unto his sentence with what patience
79   Your wisdom may inform you.
POSTHUMUS   Please your highness,
80   I will from hence today.
QUEEN   You know the peril.
81   I'll fetch a turn about the garden, pitying
      The pangs of barred affections, though the king
      Hath charged you should not speak together.   *Exit.*
IMOGEN   O
      Dissembling courtesy! How fine this tyrant
85   Can tickle where she wounds! My dearest husband,
      I something fear my father's wrath, but nothing –
87   Always reserved my holy duty – what
      His rage can do on me. You must be gone,
      And I shall here abide the hourly shot

---

66 *laughed at* regarded as incredible 74 *lock . . . restraint* lock up your prison(?), lock up and restrain you (?) 76 *Marry* indeed (by the Virgin Mary) 78 *leaned unto* obeyed 79 *inform* equip 81 *fetch* take 85 *tickle* (pretend to) gratify 87 *duty* i.e., as a wife; all she fears is a divorce

Of angry eyes, not comforted to live   90
But that there is this jewel in the world
That I may see again.
POSTHUMUS   My queen, my mistress.
O lady, weep no more, lest I give cause
To be suspected of more tenderness
Than doth become a man. I will remain
The loyal'st husband that did e'er plight troth;
My residence in Rome at one Philario's,
Who to my father was a friend, to me
Known but by letter. Thither write, my queen,
And with mine eyes I'll drink the words you send,   100
Though ink be made of gall.
     Enter Queen.
QUEEN   Be brief, I pray you.
If the king come, I shall incur I know not
How much of his displeasure. *[Aside]* Yet I'll move him
To walk this way. I never do him wrong
But he does buy my injuries, to be friends;   105
Pays dear for my offenses.   *[Exit.]*
POSTHUMUS   Should we be taking leave
As long a term as yet we have to live,
The loathness to depart would grow. Adieu.
IMOGEN
Nay, stay a little.
Were you but riding forth to air yourself,   110
Such parting were too petty. Look here, love;
This diamond was my mother's. Take it, heart,
But keep it till you woo another wife
When Imogen is dead.
POSTHUMUS   How, how? Another?
You gentle gods, give me but this I have,
And cere up my embracements from a next   116
With bonds of death!

---

105 *buy* accept as benefits (i.e., in his eyes she can do no wrong) 116 *cere up* shroud for burial (with waxed cloth; possible pun on "sealing with wax")

   [Puts on the ring.] Remain, remain thou here
118 While sense can keep it on. And, sweetest, fairest,
  As I my poor self did exchange for you
120 To your so infinite loss, so in our trifles
121 I still win of you. For my sake wear this.
  It is a manacle of love; I'll place it
  Upon this fairest prisoner.
   [Puts a bracelet on her arm.]
IMOGEN   O the gods!
  When shall we see again?
   Enter Cymbeline and Lords.
POSTHUMUS   Alack, the king!
CYMBELINE
125 Thou basest thing, avoid hence, from my sight!
126 If after this command thou fraught the court
  With thy unworthiness, thou diest. Away!
  Thou'rt poison to my blood.
POSTHUMUS   The gods protect you,
129 And bless the good remainders of the court.
130 I am gone.   *Exit.*
IMOGEN There cannot be a pinch in death
  More sharp than this is.
CYMBELINE   O disloyal thing
132 That shouldst repair my youth, thou heap'st
133 A year's age on me.
IMOGEN   I beseech you, sir,
  Harm not yourself with your vexation.
135 I am senseless of your wrath; a touch more rare
136 Subdues all pangs, all fears.
CYMBELINE   Past grace? obedience?

---

118 *sense* ability to feel, senses 121 *still* always 125 *avoid* go 126 *fraught* burden 129 *remainders of* those who remain at 130 *pinch* pang 132 *repair* restore 133 *A year's age* (perhaps "A years' age" – i.e., an age of years – is preferable) 135 *am senseless of* do not feel; *touch more rare* more painful feeling (i.e., parting from Posthumus) 136 *grace* duty

IMOGEN
   Past hope, and in despair; that way, past grace.   137
CYMBELINE
   That might'st have had the sole son of my queen.
IMOGEN
   O blessed that I might not! I chose an eagle
   And did avoid a puttock.   140
CYMBELINE
   Thou took'st a beggar, wouldst have made my throne
   A seat for baseness.
IMOGEN   No, I rather added
   A luster to it.
CYMBELINE   O thou vile one!
IMOGEN   Sir,
   It is your fault that I have loved Posthumus.
   You bred him as my playfellow, and he is
   A man worth any woman; overbuys me   146
   Almost the sum he pays.
CYMBELINE   What, art thou mad?
IMOGEN
   Almost, sir. Heaven restore me! Would I were
   A neatherd's daughter, and my Leonatus   149
   Our neighbor shepherd's son.   *150*
     Enter Queen.
CYMBELINE   Thou foolish thing!
   [To Queen]
   They were again together. You have done
   Not after our command. Away with her
   And pen her up.   153
QUEEN   Beseech your patience. Peace,
   Dear lady daughter, peace! Sweet sovereign,

---

137 *grace* heavenly grace (because she has despaired) **140** *puttock* kite (bird of prey; a term of contempt) **146–47** *overbuys . . . pays* what he pays (either in giving himself or in suffering punishment) almost entirely exceeds my value **149** *neatherd* cowherd **153** *Beseech* I beg

Leave us to ourselves, and make yourself some comfort
156   Out of your best advice.
CYMBELINE   Nay, let her languish
A drop of blood a day and, being aged,
158   Die of this folly.   *Exit [with Lords].*
    Enter Pisanio.
QUEEN   Fie, you must give way.
Here is your servant. How now, sir? What news?
PISANIO
160   My lord your son drew on my master.
QUEEN   Ha!
No harm, I trust, is done?
PISANIO   There might have been
But that my master rather played than fought
163   And had no help of anger. They were parted
By gentlemen at hand.
QUEEN   I am very glad on't.
IMOGEN
165   Your son's my father's friend; he takes his part
To draw upon an exile. O brave sir!
167   I would they were in Afric both together,
Myself by with a needle that I might prick
The goer-back. Why came you from your master?
PISANIO
170   On his command. He would not suffer me
To bring him to the haven, left these notes
Of what commands I should be subject to
When't pleased you to employ me.
QUEEN   This hath been
174   Your faithful servant. I dare lay mine honor
He will remain so.
PISANIO   I humbly thank your highness.

---

156 *advice* consideration; *languish* pine away **158** *Fie . . . way* (possibly said to Cymbeline's back to impress Imogen) **160** *drew on* (with his sword) **163** *had . . . anger* was not angry enough to fight seriously **165** *takes his part* acts as expected (?), takes his side (?) **167** *in Afric* in a desert **170** *suffer* permit **174** *lay* wager

QUEEN
  Pray walk awhile.
IMOGEN   *[To Pisanio]*
  About some half-hour hence pray you speak with me.
  You shall at least go see my lord aboard.
  For this time leave me.   *Exeunt.*

                            *

❧ **I.2** *Enter Cloten and two Lords.*

FIRST LORD   Sir, I would advise you to shift a shirt; the   1
  violence of action hath made you reek as a sacrifice.   2
  Where air comes out, air comes in; there's none abroad   3
  so wholesome as that you vent.
CLOTEN   If my shirt were bloody, then to shift it. Have I
  hurt him?
SECOND LORD   *[Aside]* No, faith, not so much as his patience.
FIRST LORD   Hurt him? His body's a passable carcass if he   9
  be not hurt. It is a thoroughfare for steel if it be not   10
  hurt.
SECOND LORD   *[Aside]* His steel was in debt. It went o'   12
  th' backside the town.
CLOTEN   The villain would not stand me.   14
SECOND LORD   *[Aside]* No, but he fled forward still,
  toward your face.
FIRST LORD   Stand you? You have land enough of your
  own, but he added to your having, gave you some
  ground.
SECOND LORD   *[Aside]* As many inches as you have   20
  oceans. Puppies!   21
CLOTEN   I would they had not come between us.

I.2   1 *shift* change   **2** *reek* give off vapors   **3** *abroad* outside you   **9** *passable*
(1) pretty good, (2) able to be stabbed through   **12** *was in debt* i.e., paid
back nothing   **12–13** *went . . . town* (like a debtor taking a back road; i.e.,
the rapier missed)   **14** *stand me* stand his ground in front of me   **21** *Puppies*
young fools

SECOND LORD   *[Aside]* So would I, till you had measured
how long a fool you were upon the ground.

CLOTEN   And that she should love this fellow and refuse
me!

27 SECOND LORD   *[Aside]* If it be a sin to make a true election, she is damned.

FIRST LORD   Sir, as I told you always, her beauty and her
30 brain go not together. She's a good sign, but I have seen
small reflection of her wit.

SECOND LORD   *[Aside]* She shines not upon fools, lest the
reflection should hurt her.

CLOTEN   Come, I'll to my chamber. Would there had
been some hurt done!

SECOND LORD   *[Aside]* I wish not so – unless it had been
the fall of an ass, which is no great hurt.

CLOTEN   You'll go with us?

FIRST LORD   I'll attend your lordship.

40 CLOTEN   Nay, come, let's go together.

SECOND LORD   Well, my lord.   *Exeunt.*

∗

∞ **I.3** *Enter Imogen and Pisanio.*

IMOGEN
I would thou grew'st unto the shores o' th' haven
2 And questionedst every sail. If he should write
And I not have it, 'twere a paper lost
As offered mercy is. What was the last
That he spake to thee?

PISANIO   It was his queen, his queen.

IMOGEN
Then waved his handkerchief?

27–28 *election* choice (punning on its theological sense of "saved")   **30** *sign*
appearance
 I.3 2–4 *If . . . mercy is* loss of a letter would be like loss of mercy (offered
by heaven or by king)

PISANIO   And kissed it, madam.

IMOGEN
  Senseless linen, happier therein than I!   7
  And that was all?

PISANIO   No, madam. For so long
  As he could make me with this eye or ear
  Distinguish him from others, he did keep   10
  The deck, with glove or hat or handkerchief
  Still waving, as the fits and stirs of's mind
  Could best express how slow his soul sailed on,
  How swift his ship.

IMOGEN   Thou shouldst have made him
  As little as a crow or less, ere left   15
  To aftereye him.

PISANIO   Madam, so I did.

IMOGEN
  I would have broke mine eyestrings, cracked them but
  To look upon him till the diminution
  Of space had pointed him sharp as my needle;
  Nay, followed him till he had melted from   20
  The smallness of a gnat to air, and then
  Have turned mine eye and wept. But, good Pisanio,
  When shall we hear from him?

PISANIO   Be assured, madam,
  With his next vantage.   24

IMOGEN
  I did not take my leave of him, but had
  Most pretty things to say. Ere I could tell him
  How I would think on him at certain hours
  Such thoughts and such; or I could make him swear
  The shes of Italy should not betray
  Mine interest and his honor; or have charged him   30
  At the sixth hour of morn, at noon, at midnight,

---

7 *Senseless* without feeling   **15–16** *ere . . . aftereye* before you stopped gazing after   **24** *next vantage* first opportunity

32   T' encounter me with orisons, for then
        I am in heaven for him; or ere I could
        Give him that parting kiss which I had set
35   Betwixt two charming words – comes in my father,
36   And like the tyrannous breathing of the north
        Shakes all our buds from growing.
          Enter a Lady.

LADY   The queen, madam,
      Desires your highness' company.

IMOGEN
      Those things I bid you do, get them dispatched.
40   I will attend the queen.

PISANIO   Madam, I shall.   *Exeunt.*

                       *

∾ **I.4** *Enter Philario, Iachimo, a Frenchman,*
      a Dutchman, and a Spaniard.

IACHIMO   Believe it, sir, I have seen him in Britain. He
2   was then of a crescent note, expected to prove so wor-
    thy as since he hath been allowed the name of. But I
4   could then have looked on him without the help of ad-
    miration, though the catalogue of his endowments had
6   been tabled by his side and I to peruse him by items.

PHILARIO   You speak of him when he was less furnished
8   than now he is with that which makes him both with-
    out and within.

10 FRENCHMAN   I have seen him in France. We had very
11 many there could behold the sun with as firm eyes as he.

IACHIMO   This matter of marrying his king's daughter,
    wherein he must be weighed rather by her value than

---

32 *encounter . . . orisons* join me in prayers   35 *charming* magical, protecting
like a charm   36 *north* north wind

I.4 Rome: the house of Philario   2 *crescent note* growing fame   4–5
without . . . admiration without feeling astonishment   6 *tabled* set down in a
list   8 *makes* is the making of   11 *behold the sun* (as eagles were supposed to
do; a metaphor for distinction; cf. I.1.139–40)

his own, words him, I doubt not, a great deal from the   14
matter.

FRENCHMAN   And then his banishment.

IACHIMO   Ay, and the approbation of those that weep
this lamentable divorce under her colors are wonder-   18
fully to extend him, be it but to fortify her judgment,   19
which else an easy battery might lay flat for taking a   20
beggar without less quality. But how comes it he is to   21
sojourn with you? How creeps acquaintance?   22

PHILARIO   His father and I were soldiers together, to
whom I have been often bound for no less than my life.
        Enter Posthumus.
Here comes the Briton. Let him be so entertained
amongst you as suits with gentlemen of your knowing to
a stranger of his quality. I beseech you all be better known
to this gentleman, whom I commend to you as a noble
friend of mine. How worthy he is I will leave to appear
hereafter, rather than story him in his own hearing.   30

FRENCHMAN   Sir, we have known together in Orleans.   31

POSTHUMUS   Since when I have been debtor to you for
courtesies which I will be ever to pay and yet pay still.   33

FRENCHMAN   Sir, you o'errate my poor kindness. I was
glad I did atone my countryman and you. It had been   35
pity you should have been put together with so mortal   36
a purpose as then each bore, upon importance of so   37
slight and trivial a nature.

POSTHUMUS   By your pardon, sir, I was then a young
traveler; rather shunned to go even with what I heard   40

14–15 *words . . . matter* gives an account of him that goes beyond the truth
18 *under her colors* as supporters of Imogen   **18–19** *are . . . him* have the effect of greatly enlarging his reputation   **19** *fortify* strengthen   **21** *without*
i.e., with (in effect, a double negative); *quality* rank   **22** *creeps* (suggests
"worming his way in")   **30** *story* tell about   **31** *known together* been acquainted   **33** *ever . . . still* always owing even though I keep paying all the
time   **35** *atone* reconcile   **36** *put together* i.e., in a duel; *mortal* fatal   **37** *importance* a matter   **40** *shunned . . . even* declined to agree (cf. "go along
with")

than in my every action to be guided by others' experi-
42   ences. But upon my mended judgment, if I offend not
to say it is mended, my quarrel was not altogether
slight.

45 FRENCHMAN   Faith, yes, to be put to the arbitrament of
swords, and by such two that would by all likelihood
47   have confounded one the other or have fall'n both.

IACHIMO   Can we with manners ask what was the difference?

50 FRENCHMAN   Safely, I think. 'Twas a contention in pub-
51   lic, which may without contradiction suffer the report.
It was much like an argument that fell out last night,
53   where each of us fell in praise of our country mistresses;
54   this gentleman at that time vouching – and upon warrant of bloody affirmation – his to be more fair, vir-
56   tuous, wise, chaste, constant, qualified, and less
57   attemptable than any the rarest of our ladies in France.

IACHIMO   That lady is not now living, or this gentle-
59   man's opinion, by this, worn out.

60 POSTHUMUS   She holds her virtue still, and I my mind.

IACHIMO   You must not so far prefer her 'fore ours of
Italy.

POSTHUMUS   Being so far provoked as I was in France, I
64   would abate her nothing, though I profess myself her
65   adorer, not her friend.

66 IACHIMO   As fair and as good – a kind of hand-in-hand
comparison – had been something too fair and too
68   good for any lady in Britain. If she went before others I

---

42 *mended* improved   45 *arbitrament* settlement   47 *confounded* destroyed
51 *without . . . report* without objection be reported   53 *our country mistresses* loved women of our countries (also "the women we have sex with,"
punning on "country" as "cunt")   54–55 *warrant . . . affirmation* pledge to
support by shedding blood   56 *qualified* having good qualities   57 *attemptable* vulnerable to seduction   59 *by . . . out* by now exhausted and changed
60 *mind* opinion   64 *abate her* lower her value (cf. "downgrade")   65 *friend*
sexual partner   66 *hand-in-hand* claiming equality   68 *went before* were superior to

have seen, as that diamond of yours outlusters many I
have beheld, I could not but believe she excelled many;   70
but I have not seen the most precious diamond that is,
nor you the lady.

POSTHUMUS   I praised her as I rated her. So do I my   73
stone.

IACHIMO   What do you esteem it at?

POSTHUMUS   More than the world enjoys.   76

IACHIMO   Either your unparagoned mistress is dead, or
she's outprized by a trifle.   78

POSTHUMUS   You are mistaken. The one may be sold or
given, or if there were wealth enough for the purchase   80
or merit for the gift. The other is not a thing for sale,
and only the gift of the gods.

IACHIMO   Which the gods have given you?

POSTHUMUS   Which by their graces I will keep.

IACHIMO   You may wear her in title yours, but you know   85
strange fowl light upon neighboring ponds. Your ring   86
may be stol'n too. So your brace of unprizable estima-   87
tions, the one is but frail and the other casual. A cun- 88
ning thief or a that-way-accomplished courtier would
hazard the winning both of first and last.   90

POSTHUMUS   Your Italy contains none so accomplished a
courtier to convince the honor of my mistress, if, in the 92
holding or loss of that, you term her frail. I do nothing
doubt you have store of thieves; notwithstanding, I fear
not my ring.

PHILARIO   Let us leave here, gentlemen.   96

---

73 *rated* estimated   76 *enjoys* possesses   78 *outprized* surpassed in value   80
or if either if   85 *wear . . . title* have title to her, possess her in name   86
ponds female genitalia; *Your ring* (1) the one Posthumus is wearing, (2) your
wife's chastity (which the ring symbolizes), (3) Imogen's vulva as Posthumus's
property   87 *brace* pair   87–88 *unprizable estimations* inestimable values
(cf. "prize possessions")   88 *casual* open to accident (cf. "casualty")   92 *to
convince* as to overcome; *honor* chastity   96 *leave* leave off (drop the subject)

POSTHUMUS   Sir, with all my heart. This worthy signor, I
98   thank him, makes no stranger of me; we are familiar at
        first.
100 IACHIMO   With five times so much conversation I should
101   get ground of your fair mistress, make her go back even
102   to the yielding, had I admittance, and opportunity to
        friend.
POSTHUMUS   No, no.
105 IACHIMO   I dare thereupon pawn the moiety of my estate
        to your ring, which in my opinion o'ervalues it some-
        thing. But I make my wager rather against your confi-
        dence than her reputation; and, to bar your offense
        herein too, I durst attempt it against any lady in the
110   world.
111 POSTHUMUS   You are a great deal abused in too bold a
112   persuasion, and I doubt not you sustain what you're
        worthy of by your attempt.
IACHIMO   What's that?
POSTHUMUS   A repulse – though your attempt, as you
        call it, deserve more: a punishment too.
PHILARIO   Gentlemen, enough of this. It came in too
        suddenly; let it die as it was born, and I pray you be
        better acquainted.
120 IACHIMO   Would I had put my estate and my neighbor's
121   on th' approbation of what I have spoke!
POSTHUMUS   What lady would you choose to assail?
IACHIMO   Yours, whom in constancy you think stands so
        safe. I will lay you ten thousand ducats to your ring
125   that, commend me to the court where your lady is,
        with no more advantage than the opportunity of a sec-
127   ond conference, and I will bring from thence that
128   honor of hers which you imagine so reserved.

_____

98–99 *familiar at first* on easy terms from the first   **101–2** *get ground, go back,*
yielding (military and dueling terms as metaphors for sex)   **102–3** *to friend* as
a friend   **105** *moiety* half   **111** *abused* deceived   **112** *persuasion* opinion; *sus-*
tain will receive   **120** *put* bet   **121** *approbation* proof   **125** *commend me* give
me an introduction   **127** *conference* meeting   **128** *reserved* secure

POSTHUMUS   I will wage against your gold, gold to it.   129
My ring I hold dear as my finger; 'tis part of it.   *130*

IACHIMO   You are a friend, and therein the wiser. If you   131
buy ladies' flesh at a million a dram, you cannot preserve it from tainting. But I see you have some religion   133
in you, that you fear.   134

POSTHUMUS   This is but a custom in your tongue. You   135
bear a graver purpose, I hope.

IACHIMO   I am the master of my speeches, and would
undergo what's spoken, I swear.   138

POSTHUMUS   Will you? I shall but lend my diamond till
your return. Let there be covenants drawn between's.   140
My mistress exceeds in goodness the hugeness of your
unworthy thinking. I dare you to this match: here's my   142
ring.

PHILARIO   I will have it no lay.   144

IACHIMO   By the gods, it is one. If I bring you no sufficient testimony that I have enjoyed the dearest bodily
part of your mistress, my ten thousand ducats are
yours; so is your diamond too. If I come off and leave
her in such honor as you have trust in, she your jewel,
this your jewel, and my gold are yours – provided I   *150*
have your commendation for my more free entertain-   151
ment.

POSTHUMUS   I embrace these conditions. Let us have ar-   153
ticles betwixt us. Only, thus far you shall answer: if you
make your voyage upon her and give me directly to un-   155
derstand you have prevailed, I am no further your

---

129 *wage* wager; *gold to it* the same amount of gold   131 *You . . . wiser* i.e.,
you know her well enough to know the danger of such a bet (Posthumus denied being her lover, "friend," at l. 65)   133 *religion* (Iachimo sneers)   134
that since; *fear* (1) are in awe, (2) are afraid   135 *This* the bet, the point of
view   138 *undergo* undertake   140 *covenants* terms of agreement   142–43
here's my ring (Posthumus might hand the ring to Philario, who is supervising
the wager, or throw it down at Iachimo)   144 *lay* bet   151 *commendation*
introduction   151–52 *more free entertainment* easier reception   153 *embrace* accept   153–54 *articles* terms (of the bet)   155 *voyage* predatory expe-
dition (with sexual innuendo); *directly* straightforwardly, convincingly

enemy; she is not worth our debate. If she remain un-
seduced, you not making it appear otherwise, for your
ill opinion and the assault you have made to her
160   chastity you shall answer me with your sword.

IACHIMO   Your hand; a covenant. We will have these
things set down by lawful counsel, and straight away
for Britain, lest the bargain should catch cold and
164   starve. I will fetch my gold and have our two wagers
recorded.

POSTHUMUS   Agreed.   *[Exeunt Posthumus and Iachimo.]*

FRENCHMAN   Will this hold, think you?

168   PHILARIO   Signor Iachimo will not from it. Pray let us
follow 'em.   *Exeunt.*

                                *

∾ **I.5**   *Enter Queen, Ladies, and Cornelius.*

QUEEN
   Whiles yet the dew's on ground, gather those flowers.
2   Make haste. Who has the note of them?

LADY   I, madam.

QUEEN
3   Dispatch.   *Exeunt Ladies.*
   Now, Master Doctor, have you brought those drugs?

CORNELIUS
   Pleaseth your highness, ay. Here they are, madam.
   [Presents a box.]
   But I beseech your grace, without offense –
   My conscience bids me ask – wherefore you have
   Commanded of me these most poisonous compounds,
9   Which are the movers of a languishing death,
10   But though slow, deadly.

---

164 *starve* die   **168** *from it* abandon it
   I.5 Britain: the palace of King Cymbeline   **2** *note* list   **3** *Dispatch* do it
quickly   **9** *are . . . of* cause

QUEEN   I wonder, doctor,
  Thou ask'st me such a question. Have I not been
  Thy pupil long? Hast thou not learned me how   12
  To make perfumes? distill? preserve? yea, so
  That our great king himself doth woo me oft
  For my confections? Having thus far proceeded –   15
  Unless thou think'st me devilish – is't not meet   16
  That I did amplify my judgment in   17
  Other conclusions? I will try the forces   18
  Of these thy compounds on such creatures as
  We count not worth the hanging – but none human –   20
  To try the vigor of them and apply
  Allayments to their act, and by them gather   22
  Their several virtues and effects.
CORNELIUS   Your highness
  Shall from this practice but make hard your heart.
  Besides, the seeing these effects will be
  But noisome and infectious.   26
QUEEN   O, content thee.
    Enter Pisanio.
    [Aside]
  Here comes a flattering rascal. Upon him
  Will I first work. He's for his master,
  And enemy to my son. – How now, Pisanio?
  Doctor, your service for this time is ended;   30
  Take your own way.
CORNELIUS *[Aside]* I do suspect you, madam,
  But you shall do no harm.
QUEEN *[To Pisanio]*   Hark thee, a word.
CORNELIUS *[Aside]*
  I do not like her. She doth think she has

---

12 *learned* taught   15 *confections* compounds (drugs)   16 *meet* fitting   17
amplify my judgment increase my knowledge   18 *conclusions* experiments;
try test   22 *Allayments* antidotes; *act* action; *gather* understand   26 *content
thee* don't worry

Strange ling'ring poisons. I do know her spirit
And will not trust one of her malice with
A drug of such damned nature. Those she has
Will stupefy and dull the sense awhile,
Which first perchance she'll prove on cats and dogs,
Then afterward up higher; but there is
40 No danger in what show of death it makes,
More than the locking up the spirits a time,
To be more fresh, reviving. She is fooled
With a most false effect, and I the truer
So to be false with her.

QUEEN   No further service, doctor,
Until I send for thee.

CORNELIUS   I humbly take my leave.   *Exit.*

QUEEN
Weeps she still, sayst thou? Dost thou think in time
47 She will not quench and let instructions enter
Where folly now possesses? Do thou work.
When thou shalt bring me word she loves my son,
50 I'll tell thee on the instant thou art then
As great as is thy master; greater, for
52 His fortunes all lie speechless and his name
Is at last gasp. Return he cannot nor
54 Continue where he is. To shift his being
Is to exchange one misery with another,
56 And every day that comes comes to decay
A day's work in him. What shalt thou expect
58 To be depender on a thing that leans,
Who cannot be new built, nor has no friends
60 So much as but to prop him?
        [Drops the box. Pisanio picks it up.]
                                Thou tak'st up
Thou know'st not what, but take it for thy labor.
It is a thing I made which hath the king

---

47 *quench* cool down; *instructions* advice 52 *name* reputation 54 *being* abode 56 *decay* waste 58 *leans* begins to fall

Five times redeemed from death. I do not know
What is more cordial. Nay, I prithee take it.   64
It is an earnest of a farther good   65
That I mean to thee. Tell thy mistress how   66
The case stands with her; do't as from thyself.
Think what a chance thou changest on, but think   68
Thou hast thy mistress still – to boot, my son,   69
Who shall take notice of thee. I'll move the king   70
To any shape of thy preferment such   71
As thou'lt desire; and then myself, I chiefly,
That set thee on to this desert, am bound   73
To load thy merit richly. Call my women.   74
Think on my words.   *Exit Pisanio.*

                A sly and constant knave,
Not to be shaked; the agent for his master,   76
And the remembrancer of her to hold   77
The handfast to her lord. I have given him that   78
Which, if he take, shall quite unpeople her
Of liegers for her sweet, and which she after,   80
Except she bend her humor, shall be assured   81
To taste of too.   82
    Enter Pisanio and Ladies.
            So, so. Well done, well done.
The violets, cowslips, and the primroses
Bear to my closet. Fare thee well, Pisanio.   84
Think on my words.   *Exit Queen, and Ladies.*
PISANIO   And shall do.
But when to my good lord I prove untrue,
I'll choke myself. There's all I'll do for you.   *Exit.*

---

64 *cordial* restorative   65 *earnest* sample; token payment   66 *mean to* in-
tend for   68 *chance . . . on* good chance (this is) to change (your fortunes)
69 *to boot* in addition   71 *shape . . . preferment* kind of advancement   73
desert meritorious action   74 *load* reward   76 *shaked* shaken (in his devotion to Posthumus)   77 *remembrancer* agent whose duty is to remind (legal
term)   78 *handfast* marriage contract   80 *liegers . . . sweet* her husband's
ambassadors   81 *bend her humor* change her mind   82 *So, so* good   84
closet private room

*

∾ **I.6** *Enter Imogen alone.*

IMOGEN
    A father cruel and a stepdame false,
    A foolish suitor to a wedded lady
    That hath her husband banished. O, that husband,
4   My supreme crown of grief, and those repeated
    Vexations of it! Had I been thief-stol'n,
    As my two brothers, happy; but most miserable
7   Is the desire that's glorious. Blessed be those,
8   How mean soe'er, that have their honest wills,
9   Which seasons comfort. Who may this be? Fie!
        Enter Pisanio and Iachimo.

PISANIO
10 Madam, a noble gentleman of Rome
11 Comes from my lord with letters.
IACHIMO   Change you, madam:
    The worthy Leonatus is in safety
    And greets your highness dearly.
        [Presents a letter.]
IMOGEN   Thanks, good sir.
    You're kindly welcome.
IACHIMO   *[Aside]*
15 All of her that is out of door most rich!
    If she be furnished with a mind so rare,
17 She is alone th' Arabian bird, and I
    Have lost the wager. Boldness be my friend!
    Arm me, audacity, from head to foot,

I.6 4 *repeated* which I have recounted (in ll. 1–3) 7 *glorious* for a noble
thing (?), held by a person in high position (?) 8 *honest wills* plain desires
9 *seasons* adds relish to 11 *Change you* i.e., change your expression; I have
good news 15 *out of door* visible 17 *Arabian bird* mythical phoenix (only
one existed at a time; hence, unique)

Or like the Parthian I shall flying fight –   20
Rather, directly fly.
IMOGEN   *[Reads.]* "He is one of the noblest note, to   22
whose kindnesses I am most infinitely tied. Reflect   23
upon him accordingly, as you value your truest
                                        Leonatus."
So far I read aloud.
But even the very middle of my heart
Is warmed by th' rest and takes it thankfully.
You are as welcome, worthy sir, as I
Have words to bid you, and shall find it so   30
In all that I can do.
IACHIMO   Thanks, fairest lady.
What, are men mad? Hath nature given them eyes
To see this vaulted arch and the rich crop   33
Of sea and land, which can distinguish 'twixt
The fiery orbs above and the twinned stones   35
Upon the numbered beach, and can we not   36
Partition make with spectacles so precious   37
'Twixt fair and foul?   38
IMOGEN   What makes your admiration?
IACHIMO
It cannot be i' th' eye, for apes and monkeys,
'Twixt two such shes, would chatter this way and   40
Contemn with mows the other; nor i' th' judgment,   41
For idiots, in this case of favor, would   42
Be wisely definite; nor i' th' appetite –   43
Sluttery, to such neat excellence opposed,   44

---

20 *Parthian* mounted archer who fired backwards while fleeing 22 *note* distinction 23–24 *Reflect upon* welcome 33 *crop* harvest 35 *twinned* exactly
alike 36 *numbered* (with) numerous (stones) 37 *Partition* distinction;
spectacles eyes 38 *admiration* wonder 40 *chatter this way* speak (i.e., give
approval) for this one (Imogen) 41 *mows* grimaces 42 *case of favor* question of beauty 43 *Be wisely definite* make a wise decision; *appetite* physical
desire 44 *neat* elegant

45   Should make desire vomit emptiness,
46   Not so allured to feed.
IMOGEN
47   What is the matter, trow?
IACHIMO   The cloyèd will –
      That satiate yet unsatisfied desire, that tub
49   Both filled and running – ravening first the lamb,
50   Longs after for the garbage.
IMOGEN   What, dear sir,
51   Thus raps you? Are you well?
IACHIMO   Thanks, madam, well.
      [To Pisanio]
      Beseech you, sir, desire
53   My man's abode where I did leave him.
54   He's strange and peevish.
PISANIO   I was going, sir,
      To give him welcome.   *Exit.*
IMOGEN
      Continues well my lord? His health, beseech you?
IACHIMO
      Well, madam.
IMOGEN
      Is he disposed to mirth? I hope he is.
IACHIMO
      Exceeding pleasant; none a stranger there
60   So merry and so gamesome. He is called
      The Briton Reveler.
IMOGEN   When he was here
62   He did incline to sadness, and ofttimes
      Not knowing why.
IACHIMO   I never saw him sad.
      There is a Frenchman his companion, one

---

45 *desire* lust; *vomit emptiness* vomit though not fed   46 *so allured* attracted
by this (i.e., by "Sluttery," l. 44)   47 *trow* I wonder; *will* sexual desire   49
running emptying; *ravening* feeding voraciously on   51 *raps* carries away   53
man's abode man to await   54 *strange* a stranger; *peevish* easily distressed   60
gamesome (hints at Posthumus's being sexually active)   62 *sadness* seriousness

An eminent monsieur that, it seems, much loves
A Gallian girl at home. He furnaces   66
The thick sighs from him, whiles the jolly Briton –   67
Your lord, I mean – laughs from's free lungs, cries "O,   68
Can my sides hold to think that man who knows
By history, report, or his own proof   70
What woman is, yea, what she cannot choose
But must be, will's free hours languish for   72
Assurèd bondage?"
IMOGEN   Will my lord say so?
IACHIMO
Ay, madam, with his eyes in flood with laughter.
It is a recreation to be by
And hear him mock the Frenchman. But heavens know
Some men are much to blame.
IMOGEN   Not he, I hope.
IACHIMO
Not he – but yet heaven's bounty towards him might   78
Be used more thankfully. In himself 'tis much;   79
In you, which I account his, beyond all talents.   80
Whilst I am bound to wonder, I am bound
To pity too.
IMOGEN   What do you pity, sir?
IACHIMO
Two creatures heartily.
IMOGEN   Am I one, sir?
You look on me. What wreck discern you in me
Deserves your pity?

---

66 *Gallian* French; *furnaces* blows forth like a furnace 67 *thick* frequent
68 *free* (also hinting at "licentious"; Iachimo's language continually hints that
Posthumus is sexually active – e.g., merry, gamesome, reveler, jolly) 72 *languish* give up to languishing (also "to being sexually frustrated") 78 *bounty*
i.e., in bestowing upon him his own qualities, and Imogen 79 *'tis* i.e.,
heaven's bounty is 80 *talents* his own qualities (?), wealth (?)

IACHIMO   Lamentable! What,
86   To hide me from the radiant sun and solace
87   I' th' dungeon by a snuff!
IMOGEN   I pray you, sir,
      Deliver with more openness your answers
      To my demands. Why do you pity me?
IACHIMO
90   That others do,
      I was about to say, enjoy your – but
92   It is an office of the gods to venge it,
      Not mine to speak on't.
IMOGEN   You do seem to know
      Something of me or what concerns me. Pray you,
95   Since doubting things go ill often hurts more
      Than to be sure they do – for certainties
97   Either are past remedies, or, timely knowing,
98   The remedy then born – discover to me
99   What both you spur and stop.
IACHIMO   Had I this cheek
100   To bathe my lips upon; this hand, whose touch,
      Whose every touch, would force the feeler's soul
      To th' oath of loyalty; this object, which
      Takes prisoner the wild motion of mine eye,
104   Firing it only here; should I, damned then,
      Slaver with lips as common as the stairs
      That mount the Capitol; join grips with hands
107   Made hard with hourly falsehood (falsehood, as
108   With labor); then by-peeping in an eye
109   Base and illustrous as the smoky light
110   That's fed with stinking tallow – it were fit

---

86 *solace* find pleasure   87 *snuff* smoking candle (see ll. 108–9)   92 *office*
duty   95 *doubting* fearing   97 *timely knowing* if one knows in time   98
then is then; *discover* reveal   99 *spur and stop* prod on (toward disclosure)
and stop   104 *Firing* giving fire to   107–8 *as / With* as if made hard by
108 *by-peeping* looking sidelong   109 *illustrous* not lustrous

That all the plagues of hell should at one time
Encounter such revolt.   112

IMOGEN   My lord, I fear,
Has forgot Britain.   113

IACHIMO   And himself. Not I
Inclined to this intelligence pronounce
The beggary of his change, but 'tis your graces   115
That from my mutest conscience to my tongue   116
Charms this report out.

IMOGEN   Let me hear no more.

IACHIMO
O dearest soul, your cause doth strike my heart
With pity that doth make me sick. A lady
So fair, and fastened to an empery   120
Would make the great'st king double, to be partnered   121
With tomboys hired with that self exhibition   122
Which your own coffers yield; with diseased ventures   123
That play with all infirmities for gold   124
Which rottenness can lend nature; such boiled stuff   125
As well might poison poison! Be revenged,
Or she that bore you was no queen, and you
Recoil from your great stock.   128

IMOGEN   Revenged?
How should I be revenged? If this be true –
As I have such a heart that both mine ears   130
Must not in haste abuse – if it be true,
How should I be revenged?

---

112 *Encounter such revolt* come upon (as a punishment) such inconstancy
113–14 *Not . . . pronounce* though not inclined to give this news, I report
115 *beggary* meanness, worthlessness, poverty 116 *mutest conscience* most
silent knowledge 120–21 *empery / Would* empire which would 121–22
partnered / With tomboys shared with whores 122 *that self exhibition* the very
allowance money 123 *ventures* commercial speculations 124 *play* gamble,
toy 125 *Which* i.e., infirmities; *boiled stuff* i.e., women treated for venereal
disease by sweating 128 *Recoil . . . stock* fall away from (what is natural to)
your royal heredity

IACHIMO   Should he make me
Live like Diana's priest betwixt cold sheets,
134 Whiles he is vaulting variable ramps,
135 In your despite, upon your purse? Revenge it.
I dedicate myself to your sweet pleasure,
137 More noble than that runagate to your bed,
138 And will continue fast to your affection,
139 Still close as sure.
IMOGEN   What ho, Pisanio!
IACHIMO
140 Let me my service tender on your lips.
IMOGEN
Away, I do condemn mine ears that have
142 So long attended thee. If thou wert honorable,
Thou wouldst have told this tale for virtue, not
For such an end thou seek'st, as base as strange.
Thou wrong'st a gentleman who is as far
From thy report as thou from honor, and
Solicits here a lady that disdains
Thee and the devil alike. What ho, Pisanio!
The king my father shall be made acquainted
150 Of thy assault. If he shall think it fit
151 A saucy stranger in his court to mart
152 As in a Romish stew and to expound
153 His beastly mind to us, he hath a court
He little cares for and a daughter who
He not respects at all. What ho, Pisanio!
IACHIMO
O happy Leonatus! I may say
157 The credit that thy lady hath of thee
158 Deserves thy trust, and thy most perfect goodness

---

134 *vaulting variable ramps* having sex with various whores   135 *In your despite* in contempt of you   137 *runagate to* renegade from   138 *fast* firm
139 *close* secret   142 *attended* listened to   151 *saucy* impudent; *to mart* should bargain   152 *stew* brothel   153 *beastly* like a beast   157 *credit . . . of* faith . . . in   158 *goodness* integrity (deserves)

Her assured credit. Blessèd live you long,
A lady to the worthiest sir that ever   160
Country called his, and you his mistress, only   161
For the most worthiest fit. Give me your pardon.
I have spoke this to know if your affiance   163
Were deeply rooted, and shall make your lord
That which he is, new o'er; and he is one   165
The truest mannered, such a holy witch   166
That he enchants societies into him.   167
Half all men's hearts are his.

IMOGEN   You make amends.

IACHIMO
He sits 'mongst men like a descended god.
He hath a kind of honor sets him off   170
More than a mortal seeming. Be not angry,   171
Most mighty princess, that I have adventured
To try your taking of a false report, which hath   173
Honored with confirmation your great judgment
In the election of a sir so rare,   175
Which you know cannot err. The love I bear him   176
Made me to fan you thus, but the gods made you,   177
Unlike all others, chaffless. Pray your pardon.   178

IMOGEN
All's well, sir. Take my pow'r i' th' court for yours.

IACHIMO
My humble thanks. I had almost forgot   180
T'entreat your grace but in a small request,
And yet of moment too, for it concerns   182
Your lord, myself, and other noble friends
Are partners in the business.

---

161 *called his* called its own   163 *affiance* loyalty   165 *new o'er* all over
again (i.e., doubly so); *one* above all, uniquely   166 *truest mannered* most
honestly behaved; *witch* charmer   167 *societies* social groups; *into* to   171
mortal seeming human appearance   173 *try your taking* test your reception
175 *election* choice   176 *Which* i.e., who   177 *fan* winnow — i.e., test
178 *chaffless* faultless   182 *moment* importance

IMOGEN   Pray what is't?
IACHIMO
  Some dozen Romans of us and your lord –
  The best feather of our wing – have mingled sums
  To buy a present for the emperor;
188   Which I, the factor for the rest, have done
  In France. 'Tis plate of rare device and jewels
190   Of rich and exquisite form, their values great,
191   And I am something curious, being strange,
  To have them in safe stowage. May it please you
  To take them in protection?
IMOGEN   Willingly;
  And pawn mine honor for their safety. Since
  My lord hath interest in them, I will keep them
  In my bedchamber.
IACHIMO   They are in a trunk
  Attended by my men. I will make bold
  To send them to you, only for this night.
  I must aboard tomorrow.
IMOGEN   O, no, no.
IACHIMO
200   Yes, I beseech, or I shall short my word
  By length'ning my return. From Gallia
  I crossed the seas on purpose and on promise
  To see your grace.
IMOGEN   I thank you for your pains.
  But not away tomorrow!
IACHIMO   O, I must, madam.
  Therefore I shall beseech you, if you please
  To greet your lord with writing, do't tonight.
207   I have outstood my time, which is material
208   To th' tender of our present.

---

188 *factor* agent   **191** *curious* anxious; *strange* foreign   **200** *short* not live up to   **207** *outstood* outstayed   **208** *tender* giving

IMOGEN   I will write.
Send your trunk to me; it shall safe be kept
And truly yielded you. You're very welcome.   *Exeunt.*   *210*

                              *

∿ **II.1** *Enter Cloten and the two Lords.*

CLOTEN   Was there ever man had such luck? When I   1
kissed the jack, upon an upcast to be hit away! I had a   2
hundred pound on't. And then a whoreson jackanapes   3
must take me up for swearing, as if I borrowed mine   4
oaths of him and might not spend them at my pleasure.
FIRST LORD   What got he by that? You have broke his
pate with your bowl.
SECOND LORD   *[Aside]* If his wit had been like him that
broke it, it would have run all out.
CLOTEN   When a gentleman is disposed to swear, it is   *10*
not for any standers-by to curtail his oaths. Ha?   *11*
SECOND LORD   No, my lord; *[Aside]* nor crop the ears of
them.
CLOTEN   Whoreson dog, I gave him satisfaction! Would
he had been one of my rank.
SECOND LORD   *[Aside]* To have smelled like a fool.   *16*
CLOTEN   I am not vexed more at anything in th' earth. A
pox on't! I had rather not be so noble as I am. They dare   *18*
not fight with me because of the queen my mother.
Every jack-slave hath his bellyful of fighting, and I   *20*
must go up and down like a cock that nobody can
match.
SECOND LORD   *[Aside]* You are cock and capon too, and   *23*
you crow cock with your comb on.

II.1   1–2 *I kissed the jack* my bowl touched the target (in game of bowls)
2 *upcast* final throw   3 *whoreson jackanapes* stupid bastard   4 *take me up*
take me to task   11 *curtail* cut down   16 *smelled* (pun on "rank" in l. 15)
18 *pox* venereal disease (standard oath)   20 *jack-slave* lower-class guy   23
cock (punning on "penis"); *capon* castrated cock, fool (also "cap-on," antici-
pating "comb on" = "coxcomb" in l. 24)

CLOTEN   Sayest thou?

26 SECOND LORD   It is not fit your lordship should under-
27 take every companion that you give offense to.

28 CLOTEN   No, I know that, but it is fit I should commit
offense to my inferiors.

30 SECOND LORD   Ay, it is fit for your lordship only.

CLOTEN   Why, so I say.

FIRST LORD   Did you hear of a stranger that's come to
court tonight?

CLOTEN   A stranger, and I not know on't?

SECOND LORD   *[Aside]* He's a strange fellow himself, and
knows it not.

FIRST LORD   There's an Italian come, and, 'tis thought,
one of Leonatus' friends.

CLOTEN   Leonatus? A banished rascal, and he's another,
40 whatsoever he be. Who told you of this stranger?

FIRST LORD   One of your lordship's pages.

CLOTEN   Is it fit I went to look upon him? Is there no
43 derogation in't?

44 SECOND LORD   You cannot derogate, my lord.

CLOTEN   Not easily, I think.

SECOND LORD   *[Aside]* You are a fool granted; therefore
47 your issues, being foolish, do not derogate.

CLOTEN   Come, I'll go see this Italian. What I have lost
today at bowls I'll win tonight of him. Come, go.

50 SECOND LORD   I'll attend your lordship.
                              Exit [Cloten with First Lord].
That such a crafty devil as is his mother
Should yield the world this ass! A woman that
53 Bears all down with her brain, and this her son
54 Cannot take two from twenty, for his heart,
And leave eighteen. Alas, poor princess,

26–27 *undertake* take on   27 *companion* fellow (term of contempt)   28–29
commit offense attack (with pun on "shit on")   43 *derogation* loss of dignity
44 *cannot derogate* i.e., have no dignity to lose   47 *issues* acts   53 *Bears all
down* triumphs over everything   54 *for his heart* for the life of him

Thou divine Imogen, what thou endur'st,
Betwixt a father by thy stepdame governed,
A mother hourly coining plots, a wooer
More hateful than the foul expulsion is
Of thy dear husband, than that horrid act   60
Of the divorce he'd make. The heavens hold firm
The walls of thy dear honor, keep unshaked
That temple, thy fair mind, that thou mayst stand,
T' enjoy thy banished lord and this great land!   *Exit.*

*

∾ **II.2** *Enter Imogen in her bed. [A trunk.]*

IMOGEN
    Who's there? My woman Helen?   *[Enter Helen.]*
HELEN   Please you, madam.
IMOGEN
    What hour is it?
HELEN   Almost midnight, madam.
IMOGEN
    I have read three hours then. Mine eyes are weak.
    Fold down the leaf where I have left. To bed.
    Take not away the taper, leave it burning;
    And if thou canst awake by four o' th' clock,
    I prithee call me. Sleep hath seized me wholly.
                                [Exit Helen.]
    To your protection I commend me, gods.
    From fairies and the tempters of the night   9
    Guard me, beseech ye!   10
        Sleeps. Iachimo [comes] from the trunk.
IACHIMO
    The crickets sing, and man's o'erlabored sense   11

II.2 s.d. *Enter . . . bed* (the bed is pushed onto the stage from the tiring
house with Imogen already in it); *A trunk* (Iachimo's trunk must be brought
onto the stage, either by being carried on or raised through a trapdoor)
9 *fairies* i.e., evil fairies   11 *o'erlabored* overworked, worn-out

12 Repairs itself by rest. Our Tarquin thus
13 Did softly press the rushes ere he wakened
14 The chastity he wounded. Cytherea,
15 How bravely thou becom'st thy bed, fresh lily,
    And whiter than the sheets! That I might touch!
    But kiss, one kiss! Rubies unparagoned,
18 How dearly they do't! 'Tis her breathing that
    Perfumes the chamber thus. The flame o' th' taper
20 Bows toward her and would underpeep her lids
    To see th' enclosèd lights, now canopied
22 Under these windows, white and azure-laced
23 With blue of heaven's own tinct. But my design:
    To note the chamber. I will write all down:
    Such and such pictures; there the window; such
26 Th' adornment of her bed; the arras, figures,
27 Why, such and such; and the contents o' th' story.
28 Ah, but some natural notes about her body
29 Above ten thousand meaner movables
30 Would testify, t' enrich mine inventory.
31 O sleep, thou ape of death, lie dull upon her.
32 And be her sense but as a monument,
    Thus in a chapel lying. Come off, come off –
        [Takes off her bracelet.]
34 As slippery as the Gordian knot was hard.
    'Tis mine, and this will witness outwardly,
36 As strongly as the conscience does within,
37 To th' madding of her lord. On her left breast

---

12 *Our Tarquin* Roman king who raped Lucrece   13 *rushes* reeds used as
floor coverings   14 *Cytherea* Venus   15 *bravely* finely; *lily* (emblem of
chastity)   18 *they do't* i.e., her lips (rubies) kiss each other   20 *underpeep*
peep under   22 *windows* eyelids; *azure-laced* i.e., with blue veins   23 *tinct*
hue   26 *arras* tapestry; *figures* carvings or characters depicted in the arras
27 *story* room (?), design on arras (?)   28 *notes* marks   29 *meaner movables*
less important furnishings   31 *dull* heavy   32 *monument* i.e., sculptured
human form lying horizontally on a tomb   34 *Gordian knot* Intricate knot
tied by Gordius, a Phrygian king. It was prophesied that whoever untied it
would rule all Asia, but Alexander the Great simply cut it with his sword.   36
conscience knowledge, consciousness (of Posthumus)   37 *madding* maddening

A mole cinque-spotted, like the crimson drops   38
I' th' bottom of a cowslip. Here's a voucher   39
Stronger than ever law could make. This secret   40
Will force him think I have picked the lock and ta'en
The treasure of her honor. No more. To what end?
Why should I write this down that's riveted,
Screwed to my memory? She hath been reading late
The tale of Tereus. Here the leaf's turned down   45
Where Philomel gave up. I have enough.
To th' trunk again, and shut the spring of it.
Swift, swift, you dragons of the night, that dawning
May bare the raven's eye. I lodge in fear.   49
Though this a heavenly angel, hell is here.   50
    Clock strikes.
One, two, three. Time, time!   *Exit [into the trunk].*
                    *

❧ **II.3** *Enter Cloten and Lords.*

FIRST LORD   Your lordship is the most patient man in
    loss, the most coldest that ever turned up ace.   2
CLOTEN   It would make any man cold to lose.   3
FIRST LORD   But not every man patient after the noble
    temper of your lordship. You are most hot and furious
    when you win.
CLOTEN   Winning will put any man into courage. If I
    could get this foolish Imogen, I should have gold
    enough. It's almost morning, is't not?
FIRST LORD   Day, my lord.   10
CLOTEN   I would this music would come. I am advised   11
    to give her music amornings; they say it will penetrate.   12

---

38 *cinque-spotted* with five spots 39 *voucher* proof 40 *secret* intimate fact
45 *Tereus* Thracian king who raped his wife's sister Philomela and cut out her
tongue to prevent her revealing it, but she wove the story into a tapestry 49
bare . . . eye (the raven was believed to wake at sunrise)
    II.3 2 *coldest* coolest, calmest; *turned up ace* made the lowest dice throw
(with pun on "ass") 3 *cold* depressed 11 *music* band

Enter Musicians.

13 Come on, tune. If you can penetrate her with your fin-
14 gering, so; we'll try with tongue too. If none will do, let
15 her remain, but I'll never give o'er. First, a very excel-
16 lent good-conceited thing; after, a wonderful sweet air
with admirable rich words to it – and then let her consider.

Song.

19   Hark, hark, the lark at heaven's gate sings,
20   And Phoebus gins arise,
        His steeds to water at those springs
22   On chaliced flowers that lies;
23   And winking marybuds begin
        To ope their golden eyes.
        With every thing that pretty is,
        My lady sweet, arise,
        Arise, arise!

28 CLOTEN   So, get you gone. If this penetrate, I will con-
29 sider your music the better; if it do not, it is a vice in
30 her ears which horsehairs and calves' guts, nor the voice
31 of unpaved eunuch to boot, can never amend.

                                        [Exeunt Musicians.]

Enter Cymbeline and Queen.

SECOND LORD   Here comes the king.

CLOTEN   I am glad I was up so late, for that's the reason I
was up so early. He cannot choose but take this service
35 I have done fatherly. Good morrow to your majesty
and to my gracious mother.

12, 13 *penetrate* affect deeply (punning on sexual penetration, continued in
"fingering")   14 *so* okay; *with tongue* by singing (punning on "oral sex")   15
give o'er give up   16 *good-conceited* well-ornamented (a piece of music full of
elaborate invention)   19–27 (The song may be sung by one of the musicians or by Cloten himself.)   20 *Phoebus* Apollo, as the sun, in his chariot;
gins begins to   22 *chaliced* cup-shaped   23 *winking* closed; *marybuds*
marigold buds   28–29 *consider* recompense, reward   29 *vice* flaw   30
horsehairs bowstrings; *calves' guts* fiddlestrings   31 *unpaved* without stones
(i.e., castrated)   35 *fatherly* as a father (modifies "take")

CYMBELINE
  Attend you here the door of our stern daughter?   37
  Will she not forth?
CLOTEN   I have assailed her with musics, but she vouch-
  safes no notice.   40
CYMBELINE
  The exile of her minion is too new;   41
  She hath not yet forgot him. Some more time
  Must wear the print of his remembrance on't,
  And then she's yours.
QUEEN   You are most bound to th' king,
  Who lets go by no vantages that may   45
  Prefer you to his daughter. Frame yourself   46
  To orderly solicits, and be friended   47
  With aptness of the season. Make denials   48
  Increase your services. So seem as if
  You were inspired to do those duties which   50
  You tender to her; that you in all obey her,
  Save when command to your dismission tends,   52
  And therein you are senseless.   53
CLOTEN   Senseless? Not so.
    [Enter a Messenger.]
MESSENGER
  So like you, sir, ambassadors from Rome.   54
  The one is Caius Lucius.
CYMBELINE   A worthy fellow,
  Albeit he comes on angry purpose now.
  But that's no fault of his. We must receive him
  According to the honor of his sender,
  And towards himself, his goodness forespent on us,   59
  We must extend our notice. Our dear son,   60

---

37 *Attend* wait at   41 *minion* darling (a term of contempt)   45 *vantages* fa-
vorable occasions   46 *Prefer* recommend; *Frame* prepare   47 *solicits* approaches, importunings   47–48 *be . . . season* make good use of appropriate
times   48 *denials* rejections (by her)   52 *dismission* dismissal   53 *are senseless* are not to understand (or obey)   54 *So like you* if you please   59 *his . . .
us* because of his earlier goodness to us

When you have given good morning to your mistress,
Attend the queen and us. We shall have need
T' employ you towards this Roman. Come, our queen.
                                        Exeunt [all but Cloten].

CLOTEN
    If she be up, I'll speak with her; if not,
    Let her lie still and dream. *[Knocks.]* By your leave, ho!
    I know her women are about her. What
67 If I do line one of their hands? 'Tis gold
    Which buys admittance – oft it doth – yea, and makes
69 Diana's rangers false themselves, yield up
70 Their deer to th' stand o' th' stealer; and 'tis gold
71 Which makes the true man killed and saves the thief,
    Nay, sometime hangs both thief and true man. What
    Can it not do and undo? I will make
74 One of her women lawyer to me, for
75 I yet not understand the case myself.
    By your leave.
            Knocks. Enter a Lady.

LADY
    Who's there that knocks?
CLOTEN   A gentleman.
LADY   No more?
CLOTEN
    Yes, and a gentlewoman's son.
LADY   That's more
    Than some whose tailors are as dear as yours
80 Can justly boast of. What's your lordship's pleasure?
CLOTEN
81 Your lady's person. Is she ready?
LADY   Ay,
    To keep her chamber.

_____

67 *line* i.e., with money   69 *rangers* gamekeepers (i.e., attendant nymphs, vowed to chastity); *false* turn false   70 *stand* hunter's station (with pun on "erection")   71 *true* honest   74 *lawyer* advocate   75 *understand the case* know how to carry on the suit ("case" puns on "vagina")   81 *ready* dressed

CLOTEN   There is gold for you.
  Sell me your good report.   83
LADY
  How? My good name? Or to report of you
  What I shall think is good? The princess!
    Enter Imogen.
CLOTEN
  Good morrow, fairest sister. Your sweet hand.
                               [Exit Lady.]
IMOGEN
  Good morrow, sir. You lay out too much pains   87
  For purchasing but trouble. The thanks I give
  Is telling you that I am poor of thanks
  And scarce can spare them.   90
CLOTEN   Still I swear I love you.
IMOGEN
  If you but said so, 'twere as deep with me.   91
  If you swear still, your recompense is still   92
  That I regard it not.
CLOTEN   This is no answer.
IMOGEN
  But that you shall not say I yield being silent,   94
  I would not speak. I pray you spare me. Faith,
  I shall unfold equal discourtesy   96
  To your best kindness. One of your great knowing   97
  Should learn, being taught, forbearance.
CLOTEN
  To leave you in your madness, 'twere my sin.
  I will not.   100
IMOGEN
  Fools are not mad folks.   101
CLOTEN   Do you call me fool?

---

83 *good report* (of Cloten)   **87** *lay out* expend   **91** *deep* effective   **92** *still*
continually   **94** *But that* in order that   **96** *unfold* show   **97** *knowing* knowledge (ironic)   **101** *Fools . . . folks* i.e., I am a fool to talk to you but not mad
("are" is sometimes emended to "cure"; see l. 104)

IMOGEN
    As I am mad, I do.
    If you'll be patient, I'll no more be mad;
    That cures us both. I am much sorry, sir,
    You put me to forget a lady's manners
106 By being so verbal; and learn now for all
    That I, which know my heart, do here pronounce
    By th' very truth of it, I care not for you,
    And am so near the lack of charity
110 To accuse myself I hate you – which I had rather
    You felt than make't my boast.
    CLOTEN   You sin against
112 Obedience, which you owe your father. For
113 The contract you pretend with that base wretch,
    One bred of alms and fostered with cold dishes,
    With scraps o' th' court – it is no contract, none.
116 And though it be allowed in meaner parties –
    Yet who than he more mean? – to knit their souls,
118 On whom there is no more dependency
119 But brats and beggary, in self-figured knot;
120 Yet you are curbed from that enlargement by
121 The consequence o' th' crown, and must not foil
122 The precious note of it with a base slave,
123 A hilding for a livery, a squire's cloth,
124 A pantler – not so eminent.
    IMOGEN   Profane fellow!
    Wert thou the son of Jupiter, and no more
    But what thou art besides, thou wert too base

---

106 *being so verbal* "your being so talkative" or "my being so outspoken"
110 *To ... hate* that I must accuse myself of hating 112 *For* as for 113
contract i.e., of marriage; *pretend* claim as an excuse (for not having me)
116 *meaner parties* people of a lower rank 118 *On ... dependency* with no
other consequence 119 *self-figured* self-arranged 120 *curbed ... enlargement* restrained from that freedom 121 *consequence* what follows (from
your inheritance); *foil* defile 122 *note* distinction 123 *hilding* good-for-
nothing; *for ... cloth* only fit for a servant's uniform 124 *pantler* pantry-
man; *not* not even

To be his groom. Thou wert dignified enough,   127
Even to the point of envy, if 'twere made   128
Comparative for your virtues to be styled
The underhangman of his kingdom, and hated   *130*
For being preferred so well.   131

CLOTEN   The south fog rot him!

IMOGEN
He never can meet more mischance than come
To be but named of thee. His meanest garment   133
That ever hath but clipped his body is dearer   134
In my respect than all the hairs above thee,   135
Were they all made such men. How now, Pisanio?   136
    Enter Pisanio.

CLOTEN
"His garment"? Now the devil —

IMOGEN
To Dorothy my woman hie thee presently.

CLOTEN
"His garment"?   139

IMOGEN   I am sprited with a fool,
Frighted, and angered worse. Go bid my woman   *140*
Search for a jewel that too casually
Hath left mine arm. It was thy master's. Shrew me   142
If I would lose it for a revenue
Of any king's in Europe. I do think
I saw't this morning; confident I am
Last night 'twas on mine arm; I kissed it.
I hope it be not gone to tell my lord
That I kiss aught but he.

PISANIO   'Twill not be lost.

---

127 *dignified* given honor 128–30 *if . . . kingdom* if, according to the virtue of each of you, you were made underhangman and he king 131 *preferred so well* promoted so high; *south fog* south wind, supposedly damp and unhealthful 133 *of* by 134 *clipped* embraced 135 *respect* regard 136 *How now* (Imogen suddenly notices that the bracelet is gone) 139 *sprited* haunted 142 *Shrew* curse (mild, polite oath; here used emphatically)

IMOGEN

149   I hope so. Go and search.   *[Exit Pisanio.]*

CLOTEN   You have abused me.

150   "His meanest garment"?

IMOGEN   Ay, I said so, sir.

151   If you will make't an action, call witness to't.

CLOTEN

I will inform your father.

IMOGEN   Your mother too.

153   She's my good lady and will conceive, I hope,
But the worst of me. So I leave you, sir,
To th' worst of discontent.   *Exit.*

CLOTEN   I'll be revenged.

"His meanest garment"? Well.   *Exit.*

*

∾ **II.4** *Enter Posthumus and Philario.*

POSTHUMUS

Fear it not, sir. I would I were so sure

2   To win the king as I am bold her honor

3   Will remain hers.

PHILARIO   What means do you make to him?

POSTHUMUS

Not any, but abide the change of time,

5   Quake in the present winter's state, and wish

6   That warmer days would come. In these feared hopes

7   I barely gratify your love; they failing,
I must die much your debtor.

PHILARIO

Your very goodness and your company

10   O'erpays all I can do. By this, your king

---

149 *so* i.e., not   151 *action* lawsuit   153 *my good lady* on my side; *conceive*
think, believe; *hope* expect

II.4 Rome: the house of Philario   2 *bold* certain   3 *means* approaches
5 *winter's* i.e., bitter, outcast   6 *feared* fear-laden   7 *gratify* repay   10 *this*
now

Hath heard of great Augustus; Caius Lucius   11
Will do's commission throughly. And I think
He'll grant the tribute, send th' arrearages,   13
Or look upon our Romans, whose remembrance   14
Is yet fresh in their grief.   15
POSTHUMUS   I do believe,
Statist though I am none, nor like to be,   16
That this will prove a war; and you shall hear   17
The legion now in Gallia sooner landed
In our not-fearing Britain than have tidings
Of any penny tribute paid. Our countrymen   20
Are men more ordered than when Julius Caesar   21
Smiled at their lack of skill but found their courage
Worthy his frowning at. Their discipline,
Now mingled with their courages, will make known
To their approvers they are people such   25
That mend upon the world.   26
        Enter Iachimo.
PHILARIO   See, Iachimo!
POSTHUMUS
The swiftest harts have posted you by land,   27
And winds of all the corners kissed your sails   28
To make your vessel nimble.
PHILARIO   Welcome, sir.
POSTHUMUS
I hope the briefness of your answer made   30
The speediness of your return.
IACHIMO   Your lady
Is one of the fairest that I have looked upon.
POSTHUMUS
And therewithal the best, or let her beauty

---

11 *of* from   13 *He* Cymbeline; *arrearages* overdue payments of tribute   14
Or or else, rather than   15 *their* the Britons' (as caused by the Romans)   16
Statist statesman   17 *prove* result in, turn out to be   21 *ordered* disciplined
25 *their approvers* those who test them   26 *mend upon* improve   27 *have posted*
must have sped   28 *corners* quarters   30 *your answer* (Imogen's) reply to you

34   Look through a casement to allure false hearts
        And be false with them.
IACHIMO   Here are letters for you.
POSTHUMUS
36   Their tenor good, I trust.
IACHIMO   'Tis very like.
PHILARIO
        Was Caius Lucius in the Briton court
        When you were there?
IACHIMO   He was expected then,
        But not approached.
POSTHUMUS   All is well yet.
40   Sparkles this stone as it was wont, or is't not
        Too dull for your good wearing?
IACHIMO   If I have lost it,
        I should have lost the worth of it in gold.
        I'll make a journey twice as far t' enjoy
        A second night of such sweet shortness which
        Was mine in Britain – for the ring is won.
POSTHUMUS
        The stone's too hard to come by.
IACHIMO   Not a whit,
47   Your lady being so easy.
POSTHUMUS   Make not, sir,
        Your loss your sport. I hope you know that we
        Must not continue friends.
IACHIMO   Good sir, we must,
50   If you keep covenant. Had I not brought
51   The knowledge of your mistress home, I grant
52   We were to question farther, but I now
        Profess myself the winner of her honor,
        Together with your ring, and not the wronger

---

34 *Look . . . casement* look through a window (like a prostitute) 36 *like*
likely 40 *this stone* (in his ring) 47 *easy* sexually promiscuous 50 *keep*
covenant hold to the bargain 51 *knowledge* carnal knowledge 52 *question*
dispute in a duel

Of her or you, having proceeded but
By both your wills.   56
POSTHUMUS   If you can make't apparent
That you have tasted her in bed, my hand
And ring is yours. If not, the foul opinion
You had of her pure honor gains or loses
Your sword or mine, or masterless leave both   60
To who shall find them.   61
IACHIMO   Sir, my circumstances,
Being so near the truth as I will make them,
Must first induce you to believe; whose strength   63
I will confirm with oath, which I doubt not
You'll give me leave to spare when you shall find   65
You need it not.
POSTHUMUS   Proceed.
IACHIMO   First, her bedchamber –
Where I confess I slept not, but profess
Had that was well worth watching – it was hanged   68
With tapestry of silk and silver; the story
Proud Cleopatra, when she met her Roman   70
And Cydnus swelled above the banks, or for   71
The press of boats or pride: a piece of work
So bravely done, so rich, that it did strive   73
In workmanship and value; which I wondered
Could be so rarely and exactly wrought,
Since the true life on't was –
POSTHUMUS   This is true,
And this you might have heard of here, by me
Or by some other.
IACHIMO   More particulars
Must justify my knowledge.   79

---

56 *wills* sexual desires   60 *leave* let it leave (some editors emend to "leaves")
61 *circumstances* details   63 *whose* (antecedent is "circumstances")   65 *spare*
omit   68 *watching* staying awake   71 *Cydnus* river in modern-day Turkey
where Antony and Cleopatra first met   71–72 *or . . . press* either because of
the crowd   73 *bravely* finely   73–74 *did . . . value* it was a question whether
form or content was better   79 *justify* prove

POSTHUMUS   So they must,
80   Or do your honor injury.
     IACHIMO   The chimney
81   Is south the chamber, and the chimney piece
     Chaste Dian bathing. Never saw I figures
83   So likely to report themselves. The cutter
84   Was as another nature, dumb; outwent her,
85   Motion and breath left out.
     POSTHUMUS   This is a thing
86   Which you might from relation likewise reap,
     Being, as it is, much spoke of.
     IACHIMO   The roof o' th' chamber
88   With golden cherubins is fretted. Her andirons –
89   I had forgot them – were two winking Cupids
90   Of silver, each on one foot standing, nicely
91   Depending on their brands.
     POSTHUMUS   This is her honor!
     Let it be granted you have seen all this – and praise
     Be given to your remembrance – the description
94   Of what is in her chamber nothing saves
     The wager you have laid.
     IACHIMO   Then, if you can
     [Shows the bracelet.]
96   Be pale, I beg but leave to air this jewel. See!
97   And now 'tis up again. It must be married
     To that your diamond; I'll keep them.
     POSTHUMUS   Jove!
     Once more let me behold it. Is it that
100 Which I left with her?

---

81 *south* on the south wall of 83 *likely to report* likely to speak for; *cutter*
carver 84 *as . . . dumb* like nature (in creative power) but unable to make a
sculpture speak; *outwent her* surpassed nature 85 *Motion . . . out* i.e., the
sculpture cannot move or breathe 86 *from . . . reap* learn at second hand
88 *fretted* adorned by carvings; *andirons* fire irons 89 *winking* with eyes
closed (i.e., blind) 91 *Depending . . . brands* leaning on their torches 94
nothing saves by no means wins 96 *Be pale* stay unflushed (i.e., calm) 97
up put up (i.e., in his pocket)

IACHIMO   Sir, I thank her, that.
  She stripped it from her arm; I see her yet.
  Her pretty action did outsell her gift,   102
  And yet enriched it too. She gave it me and said
  She prized it once.
POSTHUMUS   May be she plucked it off
  To send it me.
IACHIMO   She writes so to you, doth she?
POSTHUMUS
  O, no, no, no, 'tis true. Here, take this too.
    [Gives the ring.]
  It is a basilisk unto mine eye,   107
  Kills me to look on't. Let there be no honor
  Where there is beauty; truth, where semblance; love,
  Where there's another man. The vows of women   110
  Of no more bondage be to where they are made
  Than they are to their virtues, which is nothing.
  O, above measure false!
PHILARIO   Have patience, sir,
  And take your ring again; 'tis not yet won.
  It may be probable she lost it, or   115
  Who knows if one of her women, being corrupted,
  Hath stol'n it from her?
POSTHUMUS   Very true,
  And so I hope he came by't. Back my ring;   118
  Render to me some corporal sign about her
  More evident than this, for this was stol'n.   120
IACHIMO
  By Jupiter, I had it from her arm.
POSTHUMUS
  Hark you, he swears; by Jupiter he swears.
  'Tis true – nay, keep the ring – 'tis true. I am sure

---

102 *outsell* exceed in value   107 *basilisk* mythical serpent, believed to kill by
its look   110–11 *The vows . . . made* let women's vows no more bind them
to men   115 *probable* provable   118 *so* in this manner   120 *More evident*
which is better evidence

She would not lose it. Her attendants are
125   All sworn and honorable. They induced to steal it?
And by a stranger? No, he hath enjoyed her.
127   The cognizance of her incontinency
128   Is this. She hath bought the name of whore thus dearly.
129   There, take thy hire, and all the fiends of hell
130   Divide themselves between you!
PHILARIO   Sir, be patient.
This is not strong enough to be believed
132   Of one persuaded well of.
POSTHUMUS   Never talk on't.
133   She hath been colted by him.
IACHIMO   If you seek
For further satisfying, under her breast –
Worthy the pressing – lies a mole, right proud
Of that most delicate lodging. By my life,
137   I kissed it, and it gave me present hunger
To feed again, though full. You do remember
139   This stain upon her?
POSTHUMUS   Ay, and it doth confirm
140   Another stain, as big as hell can hold,
Were there no more but it.
IACHIMO   Will you hear more?
POSTHUMUS
142   Spare your arithmetic; never count the turns.
Once, and a million!
IACHIMO   I'll be sworn.
POSTHUMUS   No swearing.
If you will swear you have not done't, you lie,
And I will kill thee if thou dost deny
Thou'st made me cuckold.
IACHIMO   I'll deny nothing.

---

125 *sworn* bound (as if) by oath   127 *cognizance* identifying mark (worn by
servants to show whom they served)   128 *this* i.e., the ring   129 *hire* win-
nings   132 *persuaded well of* well thought of   133 *been colted by* had intercourse with   137 *present* immediate   139 *stain* mark, discoloration   140
stain moral flaw   142 *turns* sexual acts

POSTHUMUS

 O that I had her here, to tear her limbmeal!   147
 I will go there and do't i' th' court, before
 Her father. I'll do something.   *Exit.* 149

PHILARIO   Quite besides
 The government of patience! You have won. *150*
 Let's follow him and pervert the present wrath 151
 He hath against himself.

IACHIMO   With all my heart. *Exeunt.*
          *

∾ **II.5** *Enter Posthumus.*

POSTHUMUS

 Is there no way for men to be, but women   1
 Must be half-workers? We are all bastards,   2
 And that most venerable man which I
 Did call my father was I know not where
 When I was stamped. Some coiner with his tools 5
 Made me a counterfeit; yet my mother seemed
 The Dian of that time. So doth my wife
 The nonpareil of this. O, vengeance, vengeance! 8
 Me of my lawful pleasure she restrained
 And prayed me oft forbearance – did it with *10*
 A pudency so rosy, the sweet view on't   11
 Might well have warmed old Saturn – that I thought her 12
 As chaste as unsunned snow. O, all the devils!
 This yellow Iachimo in an hour, was't not? 14
 Or less? At first? Perchance he spoke not, but, 15

---

147 *limbmeal* limb from limb 149–50 *besides/ The government* beyond the
control 151 *pervert* turn aside
 II.5 1 *be* exist 2 *half-workers* i.e., in procreation 5 *stamped* minted
(i.e., conceived); *coiner* forger; *tools* (pun on "penis") 8 *nonpareil* one without equal 11 *pudency* modesty 12 *Saturn* (the god was thought to be cold
and gloomy – cf. "saturnine") 14 *yellow* i.e., in complexion 15 *At first* immediately

16 Like a full-acorned boar, a German one,
17 Cried "O!" and mounted; found no opposition
18 But what he looked for should oppose and she
19 Should from encounter guard. Could I find out
20 The woman's part in me! For there's no motion
    That tends to vice in man but I affirm
    It is the woman's part. Be it lying, note it,
    The woman's; flattering, hers; deceiving, hers;
    Lust and rank thoughts, hers, hers; revenges, hers;
25 Ambitions, covetings, change of prides, disdain,
26 Nice longing, slanders, mutability,
    All faults that man may name, nay, that hell knows,
    Why, hers, in part or all, but rather all.
    For even to vice
30 They are not constant, but are changing still
    One vice but of a minute old for one
    Not half so old as that. I'll write against them,
    Detest them, curse them. Yet 'tis greater skill
    In a true hate to pray they have their will;
    The very devils cannot plague them better.   *Exit.*

                            *

∾ **III.1** *Enter in state Cymbeline, Queen, Cloten, and*
    Lords at one door, and at another, Caius Lucius and
    Attendants.

CYMBELINE
    Now say, what would Augustus Caesar with us?
LUCIUS
    When Julius Caesar, whose remembrance yet

---

16 *full-acorned* full of acorns, also "with a large penis"; *German* (German
boars were reputedly fierce and strong) 17 *opposition* repulse, something
placed against him 18 *But . . . oppose* (i.e., her hymen, which she should
keep from sexual encounter) 19 *encounter* sexual intercourse 20–21 *motion . . . to* impulse toward 25 *change of prides* one extravagance after another 26 *Nice* finicky or lascivious; *mutability* fickleness
    III.1 Britain: the palace of King Cymbeline

Lives in men's eyes and will to ears and tongues
Be theme and hearing ever, was in this Britain
And conquered it, Cassibelan thine uncle,
Famous in Caesar's praises no whit less
Than in his feats deserving it, for him
And his succession granted Rome a tribute,
Yearly three thousand pounds, which by thee lately
Is left untendered.   10

QUEEN   And, to kill the marvel,
Shall be so ever.

CLOTEN   There be many Caesars
Ere such another Julius. Britain's a world
By itself, and we will nothing pay
For wearing our own noses.   14

QUEEN   That opportunity
Which then they had to take from's, to resume   15
We have again. Remember, sir, my liege,
The kings your ancestors, together with
The natural bravery of your isle, which stands
As Neptune's park, ribbèd and palèd in   19
With rocks unscalable and roaring waters,   20
With sands that will not bear your enemies' boats   21
But suck them up to th' topmast. A kind of conquest
Caesar made here, but made not here his brag
Of "Came and saw and overcame." With shame,
The first that ever touched him, he was carried
From off our coast, twice beaten; and his shipping,
Poor ignorant baubles on our terrible seas,   27
Like eggshells moved upon their surges, cracked
As easily 'gainst our rocks. For joy whereof
The famed Cassibelan, who was once at point –   30
O giglot fortune! – to master Caesar's sword,   31

---

10 *kill the marvel* eliminate the surprise (i.e., by making nonpayment the
norm)   14 *For . . . noses* (mocking Roman noses; see l. 37)   15 *resume* take
back   19 *ribbèd* enclosed; *palèd* fenced   21 *sands* i.e., quicksands   27 *ignorant* silly, inexperienced   30–31 *at point . . . to master* on the point . . . of
mastering   31 *giglot* strumpet

32   Made Lud's town with rejoicing fires bright
        And Britons strut with courage.
        CLOTEN   Come, there's no more tribute to be paid. Our
        kingdom is stronger than it was at that time, and, as I
        said, there is no more such Caesars. Other of them may
37   have crook'd noses, but to owe such straight arms,
        none.
        CYMBELINE
        Son, let your mother end.
40   CLOTEN   We have yet many among us can grip as hard as
        Cassibelan. I do not say I am one, but I have a hand.
        Why tribute? Why should we pay tribute? If Caesar can
        hide the sun from us with a blanket or put the moon in
        his pocket, we will pay him tribute for light; else, sir, no
        more tribute, pray you now.
        CYMBELINE
        You must know,
47   Till the injurious Romans did extort
        This tribute from us, we were free. Caesar's ambition,
        Which swelled so much that it did almost stretch
50   The sides o' th' world, against all color here
        Did put the yoke upon's; which to shake off
        Becomes a warlike people, whom we reckon
53   Ourselves to be, we do. Say then to Caesar,
54   Our ancestor was that Mulmutius which
        Ordained our laws, whose use the sword of Caesar
56   Hath too much mangled, whose repair and franchise
        Shall, by the power we hold, be our good deed,
        Though Rome be therefore angry. Mulmutius made our
            laws,

---

32 *Lud's town* London (after Lud, supposedly Cymbeline's grandfather and
the founder of the city)   37 *crook'd* i.e., Roman (cf. l. 14); *owe* own   40 *grip*
hold a sword   47 *injurious* insolent   50 *against all color* without any justify-
ing pretext (with pun on "collar"; note "yoke" in l. 51)   53 *we do* i.e., shake
off (some editors begin the next sentence with "we do")   54 *Mulmutius* earlier king, told about in chronicles   56 *whose* (the antecedent is "laws"); *franchise* free exercise

Who was the first of Britain which did put
His brows within a golden crown and called   60
Himself a king.
LUCIUS   I am sorry, Cymbeline,
That I am to pronounce Augustus Caesar –   62
Caesar, that hath more kings his servants than   63
Thyself domestic officers – thine enemy.
Receive it from me then: war and confusion   65
In Caesar's name pronounce I 'gainst thee. Look
For fury not to be resisted. Thus defied,
I thank thee for myself.
CYMBELINE   Thou art welcome, Caius.
Thy Caesar knighted me; my youth I spent
Much under him; of him I gathered honor,   70
Which he to seek of me again, perforce,   71
Behoves me keep at utterance. I am perfect   72
That the Pannonians and Dalmatians for   73
Their liberties are now in arms, a precedent
Which not to read would show the Britons cold.   75
So Caesar shall not find them.   76
LUCIUS   Let proof speak.
CLOTEN   His majesty bids you welcome. Make pastime
   with us a day or two, or longer. If you seek us after-
   wards in other terms, you shall find us in our saltwater
   girdle: if you beat us out of it, it is yours. If you fall in   80
   the adventure, our crows shall fare the better for you,
   and there's an end.
LUCIUS   So, sir.
CYMBELINE   I know your master's pleasure, and he mine.
   All the remain is, welcome.   *Exeunt.*   85
                          *

---

62 *pronounce* declare   63 *his* as his   65 *confusion* destruction   71 *he to seek*
since he seeks it; *perforce* of necessity   72 *keep at utterance* to defend to the
uttermost; *perfect* well aware   73 *Pannonians and Dalmatians* inhabitants of
what is now the Balkans   75 *cold* lacking spirit   76 *Let proof speak* let the
military test settle it   85 *the remain* that remains

❧ **III.2** *Enter Pisanio, reading of a letter.*

PISANIO
    How? Of adultery? Wherefore write you not
    What monsters her accuse? Leonatus,
    O master, what a strange infection
    Is fall'n into thy ear! What false Italian,
    As poisonous tongued as handed, hath prevailed
    On thy too ready hearing? Disloyal? No.
7   She's punished for her truth and undergoes,
    More goddesslike than wifelike, such assaults
9   As would take in some virtue. O my master,
10   Thy mind to her is now as low as were
    Thy fortunes. How? That I should murder her,
    Upon the love and truth and vows which I
    Have made to thy command? I her? Her blood?
    If it be so to do good service, never
    Let me be counted serviceable. How look I
    That I should seem to lack humanity
17   So much as this fact comes to? *[Reads.]* "Do't! The
      letter
    That I have sent her, by her own command
    Shall give thee opportunity." O damned paper,
20   Black as the ink that's on thee! Senseless bauble,
21   Art thou a fedary for this act, and look'st
    So virginlike without? Lo, here she comes.
      Enter Imogen.
23   I am ignorant in what I am commanded.
IMOGEN
    How now, Pisanio?
PISANIO
    Madam, here is a letter from my lord.

III.2 **7** *truth* fidelity; *undergoes* bears **9** *take in* conquer **10** *to* compared
with **17** *fact* deed **20** *Senseless bauble* inanimate trifle **21** *fedary for* confederate in **23** *am ignorant* will pretend ignorance

IMOGEN
 Who, thy lord? That is my lord Leonatus?
 O, learned indeed were that astronomer   27
 That knew the stars as I his characters;   28
 He'd lay the future open. You good gods,
 Let what is here contained relish of love,   30
 Of my lord's health, of his content – yet not   31
 That we two are asunder; let that grieve him.
 Some griefs are med'cinable; that is one of them, 33
 For it doth physic love – of his content   34
 All but in that. Good wax, thy leave. Blessed be 35
 You bees that make these locks of counsel. Lovers 36
 And men in dangerous bonds pray not alike;   37
 Though forfeiters you cast in prison, yet   38
 You clasp young Cupid's tables. Good news, gods! 39
  [Reads.]
 "Justice and your father's wrath, should he take me in 40
 his dominion, could not be so cruel to me as you, O 41
 the dearest of creatures, would even renew me with
 your eyes. Take notice that I am in Cambria at Milford 43
 Haven. What your own love will out of this advise you,
 follow. So he wishes you all happiness that remains
 loyal to his vow, and your increasing in love.   46
          Leonatus Posthumus."
 O, for a horse with wings! Hear'st thou, Pisanio?
 He is at Milford Haven. Read, and tell me
 How far 'tis thither. If one of mean affairs   50
 May plod it in a week, why may not I
 Glide thither in a day? Then, true Pisanio,

---

27 *astronomer* astrologer 28 *characters* handwriting 30 *relish* taste 31 *not* not content 33 *are med'cinable* have medicinal value 34 *physic* medicate; increase the strength of 35 *wax* i.e., in the seal of the letter 36 *locks of counsel* seals for confidential matters 37 *in . . . bonds* bound by risky contracts; *pray not alike* i.e., lovers adore wax seals, bonded men hate them 38 *forfeiters* those who break contracts 39 *clasp . . . tables* fasten love letters 40 *take* capture 41–42 *as . . . renew* that you could not restore 43 *Cambria* Wales 46 *increasing* (object of "wishes") 50 *mean affairs* trivial business

Who long'st like me to see thy lord, who long'st –
54 O, let me bate – but not like me, yet long'st,
But in a fainter kind – O, not like me!
56 For mine's beyond beyond: say, and speak thick –
57 Love's counselor should fill the bores of hearing,
58 To th' smothering of the sense – how far it is
59 To this same blessèd Milford. And by th' way
60 Tell me how Wales was made so happy as
T' inherit such a haven. But first of all,
62 How we may steal from hence, and for the gap
That we shall make in time from our hence-going
And our return, to excuse. But first, how get hence?
65 Why should excuse be born or ere begot?
We'll talk of that hereafter. Prithee speak,
67 How many score of miles may we well rid
'Twixt hour and hour?
PISANIO   One score 'twixt sun and sun,
Madam, 's enough for you, and too much too.
IMOGEN
70 Why, one that rode to's execution, man,
71 Could never go so slow. I have heard of riding wagers
Where horses have been nimbler than the sands
73 That run i' th' clock's behalf. But this is fool'ry.
Go bid my woman feign a sickness, say
75 She'll home to her father; and provide me presently
A riding suit, no costlier than would fit
77 A franklin's housewife.
PISANIO   Madam, you're best consider.

---

54 *bate* abate, tone down (the statement)   56 *thick* fast   57 *counselor* helper;
bores of hearing ears   58 *To . . . sense* and even overwhelm the hearing   59
by th' way on the way   62–64 *for . . . excuse* how to account for the elapsed
time, etc.   65 *or ere begot* i.e., before it is made necessary by what we do   67
rid get rid of, cover   71 *riding wagers* racing bets   73 *i' th' clock's behalf* i.e.,
in an hourglass   75 *home* go home; *presently* without delay   77 *franklin*
freeholder (small landowner, not a gentleman); *you're best* you had better

IMOGEN
   I see before me, man. Nor here, nor here,   78
   Nor what ensues, but have a fog in them   79
   That I cannot look through. Away, I prithee;   80
   Do as I bid thee. There's no more to say.
   Accessible is none but Milford way.   *Exeunt.*

*

∾ **III.3** *Enter [from their cave] Belarius, Guiderius, and*
   Arviragus.

BELARIUS
   A goodly day not to keep house with such   1
   Whose roof's as low as ours! Stoop, boys. This gate
   Instructs you how t' adore the heavens and bows you   3
   To a morning's holy office. The gates of monarchs   4
   Are arched so high that giants may jet through   5
   And keep their impious turbans on without   6
   Good morrow to the sun. Hail, thou fair heaven!
   We house i' th' rock, yet use thee not so hardly   8
   As prouder livers do.   9
GUIDERIUS   Hail, heaven!
ARVIRAGUS   Hail, heaven!
BELARIUS
   Now for our mountain sport. Up to yond hill;   10
   Your legs are young. I'll tread these flats. Consider,
   When you above perceive me like a crow,
   That it is place which lessens and sets off,   13
   And you may then revolve what tales I have told you
   Of courts, of princes, of the tricks in war.

---

78 *before me* i.e., the road to Milford; *Nor . . . here* i.e., neither to right nor to
left   79 *what ensues* the eventual outcome
   III.3 Wales: near Milford Haven   1 *keep house* stay in   3 *bows you* makes
you bow   4 *holy office* religious service   5 *jet* strut   6 *impious turbans* (in ro-
mances, giants were often Saracens and therefore pagans)   8 *use* treat; *hardly*
badly   9 *prouder livers* people who live more splendidly   13 *place* position;
sets off embellishes

16   This service is not service, so being done,
17   But being so allowed. To apprehend thus
      Draws us a profit from all things we see,
      And often, to our comfort, shall we find
20   The sharded beetle in a safer hold
      Than is the full-winged eagle. O, this life
22   Is nobler than attending for a check,
23   Richer than doing nothing for a robe,
      Prouder than rustling in unpaid-for silk:
25   Such gain the cap of him that makes him fine
26   Yet keeps his book uncrossed. No life to ours.
      GUIDERIUS
27   Out of your proof you speak. We poor unfledged
      Have never winged from view o' th' nest, nor know not
29   What air's from home. Haply this life is best
30   If quiet life be best, sweeter to you
      That have a sharper known, well corresponding
      With your stiff age; but unto us it is
33   A cell of ignorance, traveling abed,
      A prison, or a debtor that not dares
35   To stride a limit.
      ARVIRAGUS   What should we speak of
      When we are old as you? When we shall hear
      The rain and wind beat dark December, how
38   In this our pinching cave shall we discourse
      The freezing hours away? We have seen nothing.
40   We are beastly: subtle as the fox for prey,
      Like warlike as the wolf for what we eat.

---

16 *This* any act of   17 *allowed* acknowledged; *To . . . thus* to look at things
in this way   20 *sharded* with scaly wing covers; *hold* stronghold   22 *attending . . . check* doing service (at court) only to get a rebuke   23 *robe* i.e., of office (F's "Babe" is often emended to "bauble" rather than "robe")   25
gain . . . fine is respected by the elegant man ("makes him" is often emended
to "makes them," so that the phrase refers to their tailor)   26 *keeps . . . uncrossed* does not cross off (pay the debts in) his account book (possibly, tailor)
27 *proof* experience   29 *air's* air there is; *from* away from; *Haply* perhaps   33
abed i.e., in imagination   35 *stride a limit* cross a boundary (and thus risk arrest)   38 *pinching* confining or nipping with cold   40 *beastly* beastlike

Our valor is to chase what flies. Our cage
We make a choir, as doth the prisoned bird,
And sing our bondage freely.
BELARIUS   How you speak!
Did you but know the city's usuries
And felt them knowingly; the art o' th' court,
As hard to leave as keep, whose top to climb   47
Is certain falling, or so slipp'ry that
The fear's as bad as falling; the toil o' th' war,
A pain that only seems to seek out danger   50
I' th' name of fame and honor, which dies i' th' search   51
And hath as oft a sland'rous epitaph
As record of fair act; nay, many times   53
Doth ill deserve by doing well; what's worse,   54
Must curtsy at the censure. O boys, this story
The world may read in me. My body's marked
With Roman swords, and my report was once   57
First with the best of note. Cymbeline loved me,   58
And when a soldier was the theme, my name
Was not far off. Then was I as a tree   60
Whose boughs did bend with fruit. But in one night
A storm or robbery, call it what you will,
Shook down my mellow hangings, nay, my leaves,   63
And left me bare to weather.
GUIDERIUS   Uncertain favor!
BELARIUS
My fault being nothing, as I have told you oft,
But that two villains, whose false oaths prevailed   66
Before my perfect honor, swore to Cymbeline
I was confederate with the Romans. So
Followed my banishment, and this twenty years
This rock and these demesnes have been my world,   70

---

47 *keep* stay in   50 *pain* labor   51 *which* (the antecedent may be "pain" or
"fame and honor")   53 *fair act* fine deed   54 *deserve* earn, get   57 *report*
reputation   58 *best of note* most distinguished   63 *hangings* fruit   66–67
prevailed / Before had more weight than   70 *demesnes* regions

71   Where I have lived at honest freedom, paid
     More pious debts to heaven than in all
73   The fore-end of my time. But up to th' mountains!
     This is not hunters' language. He that strikes
     The venison first shall be the lord o' th' feast;
     To him the other two shall minister,
77   And we will fear no poison, which attends
     In place of greater state. I'll meet you in the valleys.
                         Exeunt [Guiderius and Arviragus].
     How hard it is to hide the sparks of nature!
80   These boys know little they are sons to th' king,
     Nor Cymbeline dreams that they are alive.
     They think they are mine, and though trained up thus
        meanly
83   I' th' cave wherein they bow, their thoughts do hit
     The roofs of palaces, and nature prompts them
85   In simple and low things to prince it much
86   Beyond the trick of others. This Polydore,
     The heir of Cymbeline and Britain, who
     The king his father called Guiderius – Jove!
     When on my three-foot stool I sit and tell
90   The warlike feats I have done, his spirits fly out
91   Into my story; say "Thus mine enemy fell,
     And thus I set my foot on's neck," even then
     The princely blood flows in his cheek, he sweats,
94   Strains his young nerves, and puts himself in posture
     That acts my words. The younger brother Cadwal,
96   Once Arviragus, in as like a figure
     Strikes life into my speech and shows much more
98   His own conceiving. Hark, the game is roused!

---

71 *at* in   73 *fore-end . . . time* early part of my life   77 *attends* is to be expected   83–84 *do hit . . . palaces* i.e., are elevated, aspire greatly   85 *prince
it* act like a prince   86 *trick* habit   90–91 *fly out / Into* (cf. "empathize")   91
say (parallel with "tell" in l. 89)   94 *nerves* sinews   96 *in . . . figure* with an
equally good acting out   98 *conceiving* interpretation; *roused* flushed

O Cymbeline, heaven and my conscience knows
Thou didst unjustly banish me; whereon,   *100*
At three and two years old, I stole these babes,
Thinking to bar thee of succession as
Thou reft'st me of my lands. Euriphile,   *103*
Thou wast their nurse; they took thee for their mother,
And every day do honor to her grave.   *105*
Myself, Belarius, that am Morgan called,
They take for natural father. The game is up.   *Exit.*   *107*

*

∾ **III.4** *Enter Pisanio and Imogen.*

IMOGEN
Thou told'st me, when we came from horse, the place   *1*
Was near at hand. Ne'er longed my mother so
To see me first as I have now. Pisanio, man,   *3*
Where is Posthumus? What is in thy mind
That makes thee stare thus? Wherefore breaks that sigh
From th' inward of thee? One but painted thus
Would be interpreted a thing perplexed   *7*
Beyond self-explication. Put thyself
Into a havior of less fear, ere wildness   *9*
Vanquish my staider senses. What's the matter?   *10*
Why tender'st thou that paper to me with   *11*
A look untender? If 't be summer news,   *12*
Smile to't before; if winterly, thou need'st   *13*
But keep that count'nance still. My husband's hand?
That drug-damned Italy hath outcraftied him,   *15*
And he's at some hard point. Speak, man! Thy tongue   *16*

---

103 *reft'st* robbed   **105** *her* i.e., Euriphile's   **107** *game is up* (repeats l. 98)
     III.4   1 *came from horse* dismounted   **3** *have* i.e., longing to see Posthumus   **7** *perplexed* troubled   **9** *havior . . . fear* less frightening demeanor; *wildness* panic   **10** *staider senses* more balanced feelings   **11** *tender'st* offer   **12, 13** *summer, winterly* good; bad   **15** *drug-damned* cursed by the use of drugs; *outcraftied* been too crafty for   **16** *hard point* (cf. "tough spot")

17   May take off some extremity, which to read
18   Would be even mortal to me.

PISANIO   Please you read,
      And you shall find me, wretched man, a thing
20   The most disdained of fortune.

IMOGEN *[Reads.]* "Thy mistress, Pisanio, hath played
      the strumpet in my bed, the testimonies whereof lies
      bleeding in me. I speak not out of weak surmises, but
      from proof as strong as my grief and as certain as I ex-
      pect my revenge. That part thou, Pisanio, must act for
26   me, if thy faith be not tainted with the breach of hers.
      Let thine own hands take away her life. I shall give thee
      opportunity at Milford Haven – she hath my letter for
      the purpose – where, if thou fear to strike and to make
30   me certain it is done, thou art the pander to her dis-
      honor and equally to me disloyal."

PISANIO
      What shall I need to draw my sword? The paper
      Hath cut her throat already. No, 'tis slander,
      Whose edge is sharper than the sword, whose tongue
35   Outvenoms all the worms of Nile, whose breath
36   Rides on the posting winds and doth belie
37   All corners of the world. Kings, queens, and states,
      Maids, matrons, nay, the secrets of the grave
      This viperous slander enters. What cheer, madam?

IMOGEN
40   False to his bed? What is it to be false?
41   To lie in watch there and to think on him?
42   To weep 'twixt clock and clock? If sleep charge nature,
43   To break it with a fearful dream of him
      And cry myself awake? That's false to's bed, is it?

---

17 *take . . . extremity* reduce the extreme painfulness (of the news)   18 *mortal* fatal   26 *tainted* contaminated   35 *worms* serpents   36 *posting* speeding; *belie* spread lies over   37 *states* people of national importance   41 *in watch* awake   42 *'twixt . . . clock* from hour to hour; *charge* burden   43 *fearful . . . him* dream involving fear for him

PISANIO
  Alas, good lady!

IMOGEN
  I false? Thy conscience witness! Iachimo,   46
  Thou didst accuse him of incontinency.
  Thou then lookedst like a villain; now, methinks,
  Thy favor's good enough. Some jay of Italy,   49
  Whose mother was her painting, hath betrayed him.   50
  Poor I am stale, a garment out of fashion,
  And, for I am richer than to hang by th' walls,   52
  I must be ripped. To pieces with me! O,
  Men's vows are women's traitors! All good seeming,   54
  By thy revolt, O husband, shall be thought   55
  Put on for villainy, not born where't grows,   56
  But worn a bait for ladies.

PISANIO   Good madam, hear me.

IMOGEN
  True honest men, being heard like false Aeneas,   58
  Were in his time thought false, and Sinon's weeping 59
  Did scandal many a holy tear, took pity   60
  From most true wretchedness. So thou, Posthumus,
  Wilt lay the leaven on all proper men;   62
  Goodly and gallant shall be false and perjured   63
  From thy great fail. Come, fellow, be thou honest;   64
  Do thou thy master's bidding. When thou seest him,
  A little witness my obedience. Look,   66

---

46 *Thy* i.e., Posthumus's 49 *favor* countenance; *jay* whore 50 *Whose . . . painting* i.e., produced by cosmetics, not by nature; false 52 *for . . . than* since I'm too rich 54 *seeming* appearance 55 *By thy revolt* because of thy turning away (infidelity) 56 *born* i.e., natural 58 *heard* i.e., heard to speak; *false Aeneas* (he deserted Dido, who killed herself as a result) 59 *Sinon* (who won the confidence of the Trojans by complaining of his treatment at the hands of his fellow Greeks, and was thus able to persuade them to admit the wooden horse, in which Greek warriors were concealed) 60 *scandal* discredit 62 *lay . . . men* destroy confidence in all honest men (the image is of sour dough spoiling other dough) 63 *be* i.e., seem 64 *From . . . fail* because of your huge failure 66 *witness* testify to

I draw the sword myself. Take it, and hit
The innocent mansion of my love, my heart.
Fear not, 'tis empty of all things but grief.
70   Thy master is not there, who was indeed
The riches of it. Do his bidding, strike!
Thou mayst be valiant in a better cause,
But now thou seem'st a coward.

PISANIO   Hence, vile instrument!
Thou shalt not damn my hand.

IMOGEN   Why, I must die,
And if I do not by thy hand, thou art
No servant of thy master's. Against self-slaughter
There is a prohibition so divine
78   That cravens my weak hand. Come, here's my heart –
79   Something's afore't; soft, soft, we'll no defense –
80   Obedient as the scabbard. What is here?
81   The scriptures of the loyal Leonatus
All turned to heresy? Away, away,
Corrupters of my faith! You shall no more
84   Be stomachers to my heart.
     [Takes his letters out of her bodice.]
                                    Thus may poor fools
Believe false teachers. Though those that are betrayed
Do feel the treason sharply, yet the traitor
87   Stands in worse case of woe.
88   And thou, Posthumus, that didst set up
My disobedience 'gainst the king my father
90   And make me put into contempt the suits
Of princely fellows, shalt hereafter find
92   It is no act of common passage, but
A strain of rareness; and I grieve myself

---

78 *cravens* makes cowardly 79 *Something* i.e., Posthumus's letters, which she
speaks of as if they were armor 80 *Obedient* i.e., in receiving the sword 81
scriptures letters (with pun on "Holy Scriptures") 84 *stomachers* decorative
breast coverings 87 *Stands . . . woe* is worse off 88 *set up* spur, push 92–
93 *It . . . rareness* my choice was not an everyday occurrence but the result of
a rare trait

To think, when thou shalt be disedged by her   94
That now thou tirest on, how thy memory   95
Will then be panged by me. Prithee dispatch,   96
The lamb entreats the butcher. Where's thy knife?
Thou art too slow to do thy master's bidding
When I desire it too.
PISANIO   O gracious lady,
Since I received command to do this business   100
I have not slept one wink.
IMOGEN   Do't, and to bed then.
PISANIO
I'll wake mine eyeballs out first.   102
IMOGEN   Wherefore then
Didst undertake it? Why hast thou abused   103
So many miles with a pretense? This place?
Mine action and thine own? Our horses' labor?
The time inviting thee? The perturbed court
For my being absent? whereunto I never
Purpose return. Why hast thou gone so far,
To be unbent when thou hast ta'en thy stand,   109
Th' elected deer before thee?   110
PISANIO   But to win time
To lose so bad employment, in the which   111
I have considered of a course. Good lady,
Hear me with patience.
IMOGEN   Talk thy tongue weary, speak.
I have heard I am a strumpet, and mine ear,
Therein false struck, can take no greater wound,   115
Nor tent to bottom that. But speak.   116
PISANIO   Then, madam,
I thought you would not back again.   117

---

94 *disedged* dulled (in sexual desire)   95 *tirest on* devourest (like a bird of
prey)   96 *panged* tortured   102 *wake . . . out* stay awake until my eyeballs
drop out   103 *abused* made bad use of   109 *unbent* i.e., not shooting (like a
bow)   110 *elected* chosen   111 *which* (the antecedent is "time")   115 *take* receive   116 *tent . . . that* probe that (wound) to its depths   117 *back* go back

IMOGEN   Most like,
  Bringing me here to kill me.
PISANIO   Not so, neither.
  But if I were as wise as honest, then
120 My purpose would prove well. It cannot be
121 But that my master is abused. Some villain,
122 Ay, and singular in his art, hath done you both
  This cursèd injury.
IMOGEN
124 Some Roman courtesan.
PISANIO   No, on my life.
  I'll give but notice you are dead, and send him
  Some bloody sign of it, for 'tis commanded
  I should do so. You shall be missed at court,
128 And that will well confirm it.
IMOGEN   Why, good fellow,
  What shall I do the while? Where bide? How live?
130 Or in my life what comfort when I am
  Dead to my husband?
PISANIO   If you'll back to th' court —
IMOGEN
  No court, no father, nor no more ado
  With that harsh, noble, simple nothing,
  That Cloten, whose love suit hath been to me
  As fearful as a siege.
PISANIO   If not at court,
  Then not in Britain must you bide.
IMOGEN   Where then?
  Hath Britain all the sun that shines? Day, night,
  Are they not but in Britain? I' th' world's volume
139 Our Britain seems as of it, but not in't;
140 In a great pool a swan's nest. Prithee think
141 There's livers out of Britain.

---

121 *abused* deceived   122 *singular* without equal   124 *No . . . life* (repeats
his assertion of l. 118)   128 *it* i.e., your death   139 *of . . . in't* belonging to
it but separated from it   141 *livers* people who live

PISANIO   I am most glad
　You think of other place. Th' ambassador,
　Lucius the Roman, comes to Milford Haven
　Tomorrow. Now if you could wear a mind
　Dark as your fortune is, and but disguise   145
　That which, t' appear itself, must not yet be   146
　But by self-danger, you should tread a course   147
　Pretty and full of view; yea, haply, near   148
　The residence of Posthumus, so nigh, at least,
　That though his actions were not visible, yet   150
　Report should render him hourly to your ear   151
　As truly as he moves.

IMOGEN   O, for such means,
　Though peril to my modesty, not death on't,   153
　I would adventure.

PISANIO   Well then, here's the point:
　You must forget to be a woman; change
　Command into obedience, fear and niceness –   156
　The handmaids of all women, or more truly
　Woman it pretty self – into a waggish courage;   158
　Ready in gibes, quick-answered, saucy, and   159
　As quarrelous as the weasel. Nay, you must   160
　Forget that rarest treasure of your cheek,
　Exposing it – but O, the harder heart!   162
　Alack, no remedy – to the greedy touch
　Of common-kissing Titan, and forget   164
　Your laborsome and dainty trims, wherein   165
　You made great Juno angry.   166

---

145 *Dark* unrecognizable   146 *That* i.e., her sex; *t' appear* if it be revealed
147 *tread* i.e., pursue   148 *Pretty . . . view* desirable, with good prospects;
haply perhaps (but also "happily")   151 *render* give information about   153
modesty chastity   156 *Command* i.e., her prerogative as the king's daughter;
niceness fastidiousness   158 *it* its; *waggish* roguish   159 *quick-answered*
quick in reply   160 *quarrelous* quarrelsome   162 *harder* too hard (different
editors regard this as applying to Posthumus, Pisanio, or Imogen herself)
164 *Of . . . Titan* of the sun who kisses everything   165 *laborsome . . . trims*
elaborate and tasteful attire   166 *angry* i.e., with jealousy

IMOGEN   Nay, be brief.
167   I see into thy end and am almost
      A man already.
      PISANIO   First, make yourself but like one.
169   Forethinking this, I have already fit –
170   'Tis in my cloak bag – doublet, hat, hose, all
171   That answer to them. Would you, in their serving,
      And with what imitation you can borrow
173   From youth of such a season, 'fore noble Lucius
174   Present yourself, desire his service, tell him
175   Wherein you're happy, which will make him know,
      If that his head have ear in music; doubtless
177   With joy he will embrace you, for he's honorable,
178   And, doubling that, most holy. Your means abroad –
      You have me, rich, and I will never fail
180   Beginning nor supplyment.
      IMOGEN   Thou art all the comfort
      The gods will diet me with. Prithee away.
182   There's more to be considered, but we'll even
      All that good time will give us. This attempt
184   I am soldier to, and will abide it with
      A prince's courage. Away, I prithee.
      PISANIO
      Well, madam, we must take a short farewell,
      Lest, being missed, I be suspected of
188   Your carriage from the court. My noble mistress,
      Here is a box; I had it from the queen.
190   What's in't is precious. If you are sick at sea
      Or stomach-qualmed at land, a dram of this
192   Will drive away distemper. To some shade,

---

167 *end* purpose, plan   169 *Forethinking* planning for in advance; *fit* pre-
pared   171 *answer to* match; *in their serving* with their assistance   173 *season* age   174 *his service* to work for him   175 *happy* gifted; *make him know*
convince him   177 *embrace* receive (as his servant)   178 *means* need for
money   182 *even* keep up with   184 *am soldier to* have courage for; *abide*
face   188 *Your carriage* taking you away   192 *distemper* illness

And fit you to your manhood. May the gods   193
Direct you to the best.

IMOGEN   Amen. I thank thee.   *Exeunt.*

                               *

∾ **III.5** *Enter Cymbeline, Queen, Cloten, Lucius, and
    Lords.*

CYMBELINE
Thus far, and so farewell.

LUCIUS   Thanks, royal sir.
My emperor hath wrote I must from hence,
And am right sorry that I must report ye
My master's enemy.

CYMBELINE   Our subjects, sir,
Will not endure his yoke, and for ourself
To show less sovereignty than they, must needs
Appear unkinglike.

LUCIUS   So, sir. I desire of you
A conduct overland to Milford Haven.   8
Madam, all joy befall your grace, and you.

CYMBELINE
My lords, you are appointed for that office;   10
The due of honor in no point omit.
So farewell, noble Lucius.

LUCIUS   Your hand, my lord.

CLOTEN
Receive it friendly, but from this time forth
I wear it as your enemy.   14

LUCIUS   Sir, the event
Is yet to name the winner. Fare you well.

---

193 *fit you to* dress yourself for
  III.5 The palace of Cymbeline **8** *conduct* escort **10** *office* duty **14**
event outcome

CYMBELINE
Leave not the worthy Lucius, good my lords,
Till he have crossed the Severn. Happiness!
                              Exit Lucius [with Lords.]

QUEEN
18   He goes hence frowning, but it honors us
      That we have given him cause.
CLOTEN   'Tis all the better;
20   Your valiant Britons have their wishes in it.
CYMBELINE
      Lucius hath wrote already to the emperor
22   How it goes here. It fits us therefore ripely
      Our chariots and our horsemen be in readiness.
      The pow'rs that he already hath in Gallia
25   Will soon be drawn to head, from whence he moves
26   His war for Britain.
QUEEN   'Tis not sleepy business,
      But must be looked to speedily and strongly.
CYMBELINE
      Our expectation that it would be thus
29   Hath made us forward. But, my gentle queen,
30   Where is our daughter? She hath not appeared
      Before the Roman, nor to us hath tendered
32   The duty of the day. She looks us like
      A thing more made of malice than of duty.
      We have noted it. Call her before us, for
35   We have been too slight in sufferance.
                              [Exit a Messenger.]
QUEEN   Royal sir,
36   Since the exile of Posthumus, most retired
      Hath her life been; the cure whereof, my lord,

---

18 *it honors us* it is to our credit (i.e., we have been patriotic)   20 *have . . . it*
i.e., approve our course   22 *fits* befits; *ripely* fully (cf. "the time is ripe")   25
drawn to head organized, mobilized   26 *sleepy* sleep-permitting (cf. "asleep
on the job")   29 *forward* (take) early (action)   32 *us* to us   35 *slight in sufferance* weak in tolerance (of her conduct)   36 *retired* withdrawn, unsocial

'Tis time must do. Beseech your majesty,
Forbear sharp speeches to her. She's a lady
So tender of rebukes that words are strokes,   40
And strokes death to her.
    Enter a Messenger.
CYMBELINE   Where is she, sir? How
Can her contempt be answered?   42
MESSENGER   Please you, sir,
Her chambers are all locked, and there's no answer
That will be given to th' loud of noise we make.   44
QUEEN
My lord, when last I went to visit her,
She prayed me to excuse her keeping close;   46
Whereto constrained by her infirmity,   47
She should that duty leave unpaid to you
Which daily she was bound to proffer. This
She wished me to make known, but our great court   50
Made me to blame in memory.   51
CYMBELINE   Her doors locked?
Not seen of late? Grant, heavens, that which I fear
Prove false!   *Exit. [Exit Messenger.]*
QUEEN   Son, I say, follow the king.
CLOTEN
That man of hers, Pisanio, her old servant,
I have not seen these two days.
QUEEN   Go, look after.
                              Exit [Cloten].
Pisanio, thou that stand'st so for Posthumus –   56
He hath a drug of mine. I pray his absence
Proceed by swallowing that, for he believes   58
It is a thing most precious. But for her,
Where is she gone? Haply despair hath seized her,   60

---

40 *tender of* sensitive to **42** *answered* accounted for **44** *loud* loudness
(some editors emend "loud of" to "loudest") **46** *close* to herself **47** *constrained* compelled; *infirmity* illness **50** *great court* important session of
court **51** *to blame* faulty **56** *stand'st so for* so strongly support **58** *Proceed
by* result from **60** *Haply* perhaps

Or, winged with fervor of her love, she's flown
To her desired Posthumus. Gone she is
To death or to dishonor, and my end
Can make good use of either. She being down,
I have the placing of the British crown.
    Enter Cloten.
How now, my son?
CLOTEN   'Tis certain she is fled.
Go in and cheer the king. He rages; none
Dare come about him.
QUEEN *[Aside]*   All the better. May
69   This night forestall him of the coming day!   *Exit.*
CLOTEN
70   I love and hate her, for she's fair and royal,
71   And that she hath all courtly parts more exquisite
Than lady, ladies, woman. From every one
The best she hath, and she, of all compounded,
74   Outsells them all. I love her therefore, but
75   Disdaining me and throwing favors on
76   The low Posthumus slanders so her judgment
77   That what's else rare is choked; and in that point
I will conclude to hate her, nay, indeed,
To be revenged upon her. For, when fools
80   Shall –
    Enter Pisanio.
             Who is here? What, are you packing, sirrah?
Come hither. Ah, you precious pander! Villain,
Where is thy lady? In a word, or else
Thou art straightway with the fiends.
PISANIO   O good my lord!
CLOTEN
Where is thy lady? Or – by Jupiter,

---

69 *forestall* deprive (by killing him) **70** *for* because **71** *that* because; *parts* qualities **74** *Outsells* outvalues **75** *Disdaining* her disdaining **76** *slanders* disgraces **77** *what's else rare* her other rare qualities **80** *packing* plotting

I will not ask again. Close villain,   85
I'll have this secret from thy heart, or rip
Thy heart to find it. Is she with Posthumus?
From whose so many weights of baseness cannot
A dram of worth be drawn.   89
PISANIO   Alas, my lord,
How can she be with him? When was she missed?   *90*
He is in Rome.   *91*
CLOTEN   Where is she, sir? Come nearer.
No farther halting. Satisfy me home   92
What is become of her.
PISANIO
O my all-worthy lord!
CLOTEN   All-worthy villain!
Discover where thy mistress is at once,   95
At the next word. No more of "worthy lord"!
Speak, or thy silence on the instant is   97
Thy condemnation and thy death.
PISANIO   Then, sir,
This paper is the history of my knowledge
Touching her flight.   100
    [Presents a letter.]
CLOTEN   Let's see't. I will pursue her
Even to Augustus' throne.   101
PISANIO *[Aside]*   Or this, or perish.
She's far enough, and what he learns by this
May prove his travel, not her danger.   103
CLOTEN   Humh!
PISANIO *[Aside]*
I'll write to my lord she's dead. O Imogen,
Safe mayst thou wander, safe return again!

---

85 *Close* secretive   89 *drawn* extracted   91 *nearer* i.e., to the point   92
home completely   95 *Discover* reveal   97–98 *silence ... condemnation* silence will condemn you instantly   100 *Touching* concerning   101 *Or* either
103 *travel* difficulty, trouble

CLOTEN   Sirrah, is this letter true?

PISANIO   Sir, as I think.

CLOTEN   It is Posthumus' hand; I know't. Sirrah, if thou
109   wouldst not be a villain, but do me true service, undergo
110   those employments wherein I should have cause to use
111   thee with a serious industry – that is, what villainy soe'er
       I bid thee do, to perform it directly and truly – I would
       think thee an honest man. Thou shouldst neither want
114   my means for thy relief nor my voice for thy preferment.

PISANIO   Well, my good lord.

CLOTEN   Wilt thou serve me? For since patiently and
       constantly thou hast stuck to the bare fortune of that
118   beggar Posthumus, thou canst not, in the course of
       gratitude, but be a diligent follower of mine. Wilt thou
120   serve me?

PISANIO   Sir, I will.

CLOTEN   Give me thy hand. Here's my purse. Hast any
       of thy late master's garments in thy possession?

PISANIO   I have, my lord, at my lodging the same suit he
       wore when he took leave of my lady and mistress.

CLOTEN   The first service thou dost me, fetch that suit
       hither. Let it be thy first service. Go.

PISANIO   I shall, my lord.   *Exit.*

CLOTEN   Meet thee at Milford Haven! I forgot to ask
130   him one thing; I'll remember't anon. Even there, thou
       villain Posthumus, will I kill thee. I would these gar-
       ments were come. She said upon a time – the bitterness
       of it I now belch from my heart – that she held the very
       garment of Posthumus in more respect than my noble
       and natural person, together with the adornment of my
136   qualities. With that suit upon my back will I ravish her;
       first kill him, and in her eyes. There shall she see my
138   valor, which will then be a torment to her contempt.

---

109 *undergo* undertake **111** *industry* application **114** *relief* assistance;
voice support; *preferment* advancement **118** *course* ordinary way **136**
qualities talents **138** *to her contempt* to her because of her contempt for me

He on the ground, my speech of insultment ended on   139
his dead body, and when my lust hath dined – which,   140
as I say, to vex her I will execute in the clothes that she
so praised – to the court I'll knock her back, foot her   142
home again. She hath despised me rejoicingly, and I'll
be merry in my revenge.
    Enter Pisanio [with the clothes].
Be those the garments?
PISANIO   Ay, my noble lord.
CLOTEN   How long is't since she went to Milford Haven?
PISANIO   She can scarce be there yet.
CLOTEN   Bring this apparel to my chamber; that is the
second thing that I have commanded thee. The third is   150
that thou wilt be a voluntary mute to my design. Be   151
but duteous, and true preferment shall tender itself to
thee. My revenge is now at Milford. Would I had wings
to follow it! Come, and be true.   *Exit.*

PISANIO
Thou bid'st me to my loss, for true to thee   155
Were to prove false, which I will never be,
To him that is most true. To Milford go,   157
And find not her whom thou pursuest. Flow, flow,
You heavenly blessings, on her. This fool's speed
Be crossed with slowness; labor be his meed.   *Exit.*   160
              *

∾ **III.6** *Enter Imogen alone [in boy's clothes].*

IMOGEN
I see a man's life is a tedious one.
I have tired myself, and for two nights together
Have made the ground my bed. I should be sick

---

139 *insultment* triumph and scorn **142** *foot* kick **151** *be . . . mute to* be
willing to keep quiet about (as if mute) **155** *to my loss* to lose my honor
157 *him* i.e., Posthumus, whom Pisanio thinks misled rather than untrue
160 *crossed* thwarted; *meed* reward
  III.6 Wales, near Milford Haven

But that my resolution helps me. Milford,
When from the mountain top Pisanio showed thee,
6   Thou wast within a ken. O Jove, I think
7   Foundations fly the wretched – such, I mean,
Where they should be relieved. Two beggars told me
I could not miss my way. Will poor folks lie,
10 That have afflictions on them, knowing 'tis
11 A punishment or trial? Yes. No wonder,
12 When rich ones scarce tell true. To lapse in fullness
13 Is sorer than to lie for need, and falsehood
Is worse in kings than beggars. My dear lord,
Thou art one o' th' false ones. Now I think on thee
16 My hunger's gone, but even before, I was
17 At point to sink for food. But what is this?
18 Here is a path to't. 'Tis some savage hold.
19 I were best not call; I dare not call. Yet famine,
20 Ere clean it o'erthrow nature, makes it valiant.
21 Plenty and peace breeds cowards; hardness ever
22 Of hardiness is mother. Ho! Who's here?
If anything that's civil, speak; if savage,
24 Take or lend. Ho! No answer? Then I'll enter.
Best draw my sword, and if mine enemy
But fear the sword like me, he'll scarcely look on't.
27 Such a foe, good heavens!   *Exit [into the cave].*
   Enter Belarius, Guiderius, and Arviragus.
BELARIUS
28 You, Polydore, have proved best woodman and
Are master of the feast. Cadwal and I
30 Will play the cook and servant; 'tis our match.

---

6 *a ken* sight 7 *Foundations* (pun on the meanings "security" and "charitable organizations") 11 *trial* test (of faith or moral quality) 12 *lapse in fulness* lie when well-to-do 13 *sorer* worse 16 *even* just 17 *At point* about; *for* for lack of 18 *hold* stronghold 19 *were best* had better 20 *clean* completely; *nature* i.e., a person 21 *hardness* hardship 22 *hardiness* courage, endurance 24 *Take or lend* i.e., she expects the civil person to speak, the savage to act, be it to take (life or money) or give (food or blows) 27 *Such . . . heavens* heavens grant me such a foe 28 *woodman* hunter 30 *match* bargain

The sweat of industry would dry and die
But for the end it works to. Come, our stomachs
Will make what's homely savory. Weariness   33
Can snore upon the flint when resty sloth   34
Finds the down pillow hard. Now peace be here,
Poor house, that keep'st thyself.   36
GUIDERIUS   I am throughly weary.
ARVIRAGUS
I am weak with toil, yet strong in appetite.
GUIDERIUS
There is cold meat i' th' cave. We'll browse on that   38
Whilst what we have killed be cooked.
BELARIUS *[Looking into the cave]*   Stay, come not in.
But that it eats our victuals, I should think   40
Here were a fairy.
GUIDERIUS   What's the matter, sir?
BELARIUS
By Jupiter, an angel! or, if not,
An earthly paragon! Behold divineness
No elder than a boy!
     Enter Imogen.
IMOGEN
Good masters, harm me not.
Before I entered here, I called and thought
To have begged or bought what I have took. Good troth,   47
I have stol'n nought, nor would not, though I had found
Gold strewed i' th' floor. Here's money for my meat.
I would have left it on the board so soon   50
As I had made my meal, and parted
With pray'rs for the provider.
GUIDERIUS   Money, youth?
ARVIRAGUS
All gold and silver rather turn to dirt,

---

33 *homely* plain   34 *resty* lazy   36 *keep'st* takest care of; *throughly* thoroughly
38 *browse* nibble   47 *Good troth* in truth

54   As 'tis no better reckoned but of those
Who worship dirty gods.
IMOGEN   I see you're angry.
Know, if you kill me for my fault, I should
Have died had I not made it.
BELARIUS   Whither bound?
IMOGEN
To Milford Haven.
BELARIUS
What's your name?
IMOGEN
60   Fidele, sir. I have a kinsman who
Is bound for Italy; he embarked at Milford;
62   To whom being going, almost spent with hunger,
63   I am fall'n in this offense.
BELARIUS   Prithee, fair youth,
Think us no churls, nor measure our good minds
By this rude place we live in. Well encountered!
66   'Tis almost night; you shall have better cheer
67   Ere you depart, and thanks to stay and eat it.
Boys, bid him welcome.
GUIDERIUS   Were you a woman, youth,
69   I should woo hard but be your groom in honesty.
70   I bid for you as I do buy.
ARVIRAGUS   I'll make't my comfort
He is a man. I'll love him as my brother,
And such a welcome as I'd give to him
After long absence, such is yours. Most welcome.
74   Be sprightly, for you fall 'mongst friends.
IMOGEN   'Mongst friends?
If brothers. *[Aside]* Would it had been so that they

---

54 *of* by   62 *spent* exhausted   63 *in* into   66 *cheer* entertainment   67
thanks to i.e., we'll be pleased to have you   69 *but be* but to be   70 *I bid . . .
buy* (literal meaning not clear; the idea is that he means what he says; he sets
a high value on Fidele, as in making a serious bid for purchase)   74 *sprightly*
in good spirits

Had been my father's sons! Then had my prize   76
Been less, and so more equal ballasting   77
To thee, Posthumus.   78
BELARIUS   He wrings at some distress.
GUIDERIUS
Would I could free't!
ARVIRAGUS   Or I, whate'er it be,
What pain it cost, what danger. Gods!   80
BELARIUS   Hark, boys.
    [Whispers.]
IMOGEN
Great men
That had a court no bigger than this cave,
That did attend themselves and had the virtue   83
Which their own conscience sealed them, laying by   84
That nothing-gift of differing multitudes,   85
Could not outpeer these twain. Pardon me, gods,   86
I'd change my sex to be companion with them,
Since Leonatus' false.
BELARIUS   It shall be so.
Boys, we'll go dress our hunt. Fair youth, come in.   89
Discourse is heavy, fasting. When we have supped,   90
We'll mannerly demand thee of thy story,
So far as thou wilt speak it.
GUIDERIUS   Pray draw near.
ARVIRAGUS
The night to th' owl and morn to th' lark less welcome.
IMOGEN
Thanks, sir.
ARVIRAGUS
I pray draw near.   *Exeunt.*

---

76 *prize* (pun on the meanings "value" and "captured ship")   77 *less* i.e., she
would not have been heir to the throne; *ballasting* weight, position   78
wrings writhes   83 *attend* serve   84 *laying by* disregarding   85 *nothing-gift*
worthless gift of adulation; *differing* fickle   86 *outpeer* excel   89 *dress our
hunt* prepare our game   90 *Discourse . . . fasting* conversation is burdensome
when we have not eaten

*

∾ **III.7** *Enter two Roman Senators, and Tribunes.*

FIRST SENATOR
1   This is the tenor of the emperor's writ:
     That since the common men are now in action
     'Gainst the Pannonians and Dalmatians,
     And that the legions now in Gallia are
5   Full weak to undertake our wars against
6   The fall'n-off Britons, that we do incite
     The gentry to this business. He creates
     Lucius proconsul, and to you the tribunes,
9   For this immediate levy, he commands
10   His absolute commission. Long live Caesar!
TRIBUNE
     Is Lucius general of the forces?
SECOND SENATOR   Ay.
TRIBUNE
     Remaining now in Gallia?
FIRST SENATOR   With those legions
     Which I have spoke of, whereunto your levy
14   Must be supplyant. The words of your commission
15   Will tie you to the numbers and the time
     Of their dispatch.
TRIBUNE   We will discharge our duty.   *Exeunt.*
                              *

∾ **IV.1** *Enter Cloten alone.*

CLOTEN   I am near to th' place where they should meet,
2   if Pisanio have mapped it truly. How fit his garments

III.7 Rome 1 *writ* dispatch 5 *Full* quite 6 *fall'n-off* revolted; *incite* sum-
mon 9 *commands* entrusts 10 *commission* authority 14 *supplyant* supple-
mentary 15 *tie you to* specify you
     IV.1 Wales 2 *fit* fittingly

serve me! Why should his mistress, who was made by
him that made the tailor, not be fit too? The rather, sav- 4
ing reverence of the word, for 'tis said a woman's fitness 5
comes by fits. Therein I must play the workman. I dare 6
speak it to myself, for it is not vainglory for a man and
his glass to confer in his own chamber – I mean, the 8
lines of my body are as well drawn as his; no less young,
more strong, not beneath him in fortunes, beyond him 10
in the advantage of the time, above him in birth, alike 11
conversant in general services, and more remarkable in 12
single oppositions. Yet this imperceiverant thing loves 13
him in my despite. What mortality is! Posthumus, thy 14
head, which now is growing upon thy shoulders, shall
within this hour be off, thy mistress enforced, thy gar- 16
ments cut to pieces before thy face; and all this done, 17
spurn her home to her father, who may haply be a little 18
angry for my so rough usage; but my mother, having
power of his testiness, shall turn all into my commenda- 20
tions. My horse is tied up safe. Out, sword, and to a sore 21
purpose! Fortune put them into my hand. This is the 22
very description of their meeting place, and the fellow
dares not deceive me.   *Exit.*

*

---

4 *fit* i.e., for me (with pun on the meanings "inclined to" and "have sex
with")   4–5 *saving reverence* with all due respect to you (apology to audience
for puns on "fit")   5 *for* since; *fitness* sexual inclination, sexual activity   6 *fits*
(cf. "fits and starts")   8 *glass* mirror   11 *of the time* in the present (social)
world   11–12 *alike conversant* equally experienced   12 *services* i.e., military
13 *oppositions* combats; *imperceiverant* unperceiving   14 *What mortality is*
what a thing life is   16 *enforced* raped   17 *thy face* (some editors emend
"thy" to "her")   18 *spurn* kick; *haply* perhaps   20 *power of* control over
20–21 *commendations* credit   21 *sore* painful   22 *This is* this place fits

∾ **IV.2** *Enter Belarius, Guiderius, Arviragus, and Imo-*
gen from the cave.

BELARIUS   *[To Imogen]*
You are not well. Remain here in the cave;
We'll come to you after hunting.
ARVIRAGUS   *[To Imogen]*   Brother, stay here.
Are we not brothers?
IMOGEN   So man and man should be,
4   But clay and clay differs in dignity,
5   Whose dust is both alike. I am very sick.
GUIDERIUS
Go you to hunting; I'll abide with him.
IMOGEN
So sick I am not, yet I am not well,
8   But not so citizen a wanton as
To seem to die ere sick. So please you, leave me;
10   Stick to your journal course; the breach of custom
Is breach of all. I am ill, but your being by me
12   Cannot amend me; society is no comfort
To one not sociable. I am not very sick,
Since I can reason of it. Pray you trust me here –
I'll rob none but myself – and let me die,
16   Stealing so poorly.
GUIDERIUS   I love thee – I have spoke it –
17   How much the quantity, the weight as much
As I do love my father.
BELARIUS   What? How, how?
ARVIRAGUS
19   If it be sin to say so, sir, I yoke me
20   In my good brother's fault. I know not why

IV.2   **4** *clay and clay* different persons   **5** *dust* remains after death   **8** *citizen*
city-bred (cf. "citified"); *wanton* spoiled child   **10** *journal* daily, regular;
breach disruption   **12** *amend* make better   **16** *poorly* i.e., from myself only
17 *How . . . as much* as much, as deeply   **19–20** *yoke . . . fault* confess to
having committed the same fault as my brother

I love this youth, and I have heard you say
Love's reason's without reason. The bier at door,
And a demand who is't shall die, I'd say
"My father, not this youth."   24

BELARIUS   *[Aside]*   O noble strain!
O worthiness of nature, breed of greatness!
Cowards father cowards and base things sire base;   26
Nature hath meal and bran, contempt and grace.
I'm not their father; yet who this should be   28
Doth miracle itself, loved before me. –
'Tis the ninth hour o' th' morn.   30

ARVIRAGUS   Brother, farewell.

IMOGEN
I wish ye sport.   31

ARVIRAGUS   You health.
    [To Belarius]   So please you, sir.

IMOGEN   *[Aside]*
These are kind creatures. Gods, what lies I have heard!
Our courtiers say all's savage but at court.
Experience, O, thou disprov'st report!
Th' imperious seas breeds monsters; for the dish   35
Poor tributary rivers as sweet fish.   36
I am sick still, heartsick. Pisanio,
I'll now taste of thy drug.   38
    [Swallows some.]

GUIDERIUS   I could not stir him.
He said he was gentle, but unfortunate;   39
Dishonestly afflicted, but yet honest.   40

ARVIRAGUS
Thus did he answer me, yet said hereafter
I might know more.

------

24 *strain* lineage, heredity **26, 27** (in the folio text, these lines are introduced by quotation marks to identify them as maxims or well-known say-
ings) **28–29** *who . . . me* that this person, whoever he may be, should be
loved ahead of me is miraculous **31** *So please you* at your command **35**
imperious imperial **36** *rivers . . . fish* rivers (breed) just as sweet fish (as the
sea does) **38** *stir* move (to tell about himself) **39** *gentle* of noble birth

BELARIUS   To th' field, to th' field.
      [To Imogen]
      We'll leave you for this time; go in and rest.
ARVIRAGUS
      We'll not be long away.
BELARIUS   Pray be not sick,
      For you must be our housewife.
IMOGEN   Well or ill,
46   I am bound to you.   *Exit [into the cave].*
BELARIUS   And shalt be ever.
      This youth, howe'er distressed, appears he hath had
      Good ancestors.
ARVIRAGUS   How angel-like he sings!
GUIDERIUS
49   But his neat cookery! He cut our roots in characters,
50   And sauced our broths as Juno had been sick
51   And he her dieter.
ARVIRAGUS   Nobly he yokes
      A smiling with a sigh, as if the sigh
53   Was that it was for not being such a smile;
      The smile mocking the sigh that it would fly
      From so divine a temple to commix·
      With winds that sailors rail at.
GUIDERIUS   I do note
57   That grief and patience, rooted in them both,
58   Mingle their spurs together.
ARVIRAGUS   Grow patience,
59   And let the stinking elder, grief, untwine
60   His perishing root with the increasing vine.
BELARIUS
61   It is great morning. Come away. Who's there?

------

46 *bound* obligated; *shalt be* i.e., bound (by emotional ties)   49 *neat* fine, elegant; *characters* letters (of the alphabet), designs   50 *as* as if   51 *dieter* di-
etitian   53 *that* what   57 *them* i.e., the smile and sigh (some editors emend
to "him")   58 *spurs* roots   59 *elder* elder tree (on which it was thought Judas
hanged himself)   60 *perishing* noxious; *with . . . vine* from the increasing
vine (?), as the vine increases (?)   61 *great morning* broad daylight

Enter Cloten.

CLOTEN
   I cannot find those runagates. That villain   62
   Hath mocked me. I am faint.   63
BELARIUS   "Those runagates"?
   Means he not us? I partly know him. 'Tis
   Cloten, the son o' th' queen. I fear some ambush.
   I saw him not these many years, and yet
   I know 'tis he. We are held as outlaws. Hence!   67
GUIDERIUS
   He is but one. You and my brother search
   What companies are near. Pray you, away.   69
   Let me alone with him.   70
                         [Exeunt Belarius and Arviragus.]
CLOTEN   Soft, what are you
   That fly me thus? Some villain mountaineers?   71
   I have heard of such. What slave art thou?
GUIDERIUS   A thing
   More slavish did I ne'er than answering
   A "slave" without a knock.   74
CLOTEN   Thou art a robber,
   A lawbreaker, a villain. Yield thee, thief.
GUIDERIUS
   To who? To thee? What art thou? Have not I
   An arm as big as thine? A heart as big?
   Thy words, I grant, are bigger, for I wear not
   My dagger in my mouth. Say what thou art,
   Why I should yield to thee.   80
CLOTEN   Thou villain base,
   Know'st me not by my clothes?   81

---

62 *runagates* runaways   63 *mocked* fooled   67 *held* regarded   69 *companies*
followers   70 *Soft* stop (exclamation; cf. "take it easy")   71 *mountaineers*
mountain dwellers (often criminals)   74 *"slave"* (Guiderius may be quoting
Cloten's word or simply calling Cloten a slave)   81 *clothes* i.e., court clothes

GUIDERIUS   No, nor thy tailor, rascal,
Who is thy grandfather. He made those clothes,
83   Which, as it seems, make thee.
CLOTEN   Thou precious varlet,
My tailor made them not.
GUIDERIUS   Hence then, and thank
The man that gave them thee. Thou art some fool;
86   I am loath to beat thee.
CLOTEN   Thou injurious thief,
Hear but my name and tremble.
GUIDERIUS   What's thy name?
CLOTEN
Cloten, thou villain.
GUIDERIUS
Cloten, thou double villain, be thy name,
90   I cannot tremble at it. Were it Toad, or Adder, Spider,
'Twould move me sooner.
CLOTEN   To thy further fear,
92   Nay, to thy mere confusion, thou shalt know
93   I am son to th' queen.
GUIDERIUS   I am sorry for't, not seeming
So worthy as thy birth.
CLOTEN   Art not afeard?
GUIDERIUS
Those that I reverence, those I fear – the wise;
96   At fools I laugh, not fear them.
CLOTEN   Die the death!
97   When I have slain thee with my proper hand,
I'll follow those that even now fled hence
And on the gates of Lud's town set your heads.
100   Yield, rustic mountaineer.   *Fight and exeunt.*
     Enter Belarius and Arviragus.

---

83 *varlet* knave   86 *injurious* insulting   92 *mere confusion* utter destruction
93 *not seeming* since you do not seem   96 *Die the death* (as if he were im-
posing a legal sentence)   97 *proper* own

BELARIUS
  No company's abroad?   101
ARVIRAGUS
  None in the world. You did mistake him sure.
BELARIUS
  I cannot tell. Long is it since I saw him,
  But time hath nothing blurred those lines of favor   104
  Which then he wore. The snatches in his voice,   105
  And burst of speaking, were as his. I am absolute   106
  'Twas very Cloten.   107
ARVIRAGUS   In this place we left them.
  I wish my brother make good time with him,   108
  You say he is so fell.   109
BELARIUS   Being scarce made up,
  I mean to man, he had not apprehension   110
  Of roaring terrors; for defect of judgment   111
  Is oft the cause of fear.
    Enter Guiderius [with Cloten's head].
                    But see, thy brother.
GUIDERIUS
  This Cloten was a fool, an empty purse;
  There was no money in't. Not Hercules
  Could have knocked out his brains, for he had none.
  Yet I not doing this, the fool had borne
  My head as I do his.
BELARIUS   What hast thou done?
GUIDERIUS
  I am perfect what: cut off one Cloten's head,   118

---

101 *abroad* around, in the neighborhood   104 *lines of favor* facial lines
105 *snatches* catches, hesitations   106 *absolute* positive   107 *very Cloten*
Cloten himself   108 *make good time* may succeed (cf. "have a good day")
109 *fell* savage; *made up* grown up (in sense of years or mental ability)   110
apprehension understanding   111–12 *defect . . . fear* (if Belarius is talking
about Cloten, the lines probably need emending – e.g., "th' effect" for "defect"; if Belarius is talking about Guiderius, the lines are perfectly clear)
118 *perfect* aware

Son to the queen, after his own report;
120 Who called me traitor, mountaineer, and swore
121 With his own single hand he'd take us in,
Displace our heads where – thank the gods – they grow,
And set them on Lud's town.
BELARIUS   We are all undone.
GUIDERIUS
Why, worthy father, what have we to lose
125 But that he swore to take, our lives? The law
126 Protects not us. Then why should we be tender
To let an arrogant piece of flesh threat us,
Play judge and executioner all himself,
129 For we do fear the law? What company
130 Discover you abroad?
BELARIUS   No single soul
Can we set eye on, but in all safe reason
132 He must have some attendants. Though his honor
Was nothing but mutation – ay, and that
From one bad thing to worse – not frenzy, not
Absolute madness could so far have raved
To bring him here alone. Although perhaps
It may be heard at court that such as we
Cave here, hunt here, are outlaws, and in time
139 May make some stronger head; the which he hearing –
140 As it is like him – might break out, and swear
141 He'd fetch us in; yet is't not probable
142 To come alone, either he so undertaking,
143 Or they so suffering. Then on good ground we fear,
144 If we do fear this body hath a tail
145 More perilous than the head.

---

121 *take us in* subdue us   125 *that* what   126–27 *tender / To* so tolerant as
to   129 *For* because   132 *honor* (Implies steadfastness; ironically joined
with *mutation,* changeableness. Some editors emend to "humor.")   139
make . . . head become a stronger force   141 *fetch us in* capture us   142 *To
come* for him to come   143 *suffering* permitting (it)   144 *tail* i.e., what
comes after: followers hostile to us   145 *ordinance* whatever is ordained

ARVIRAGUS   Let ordinance
  Come as the gods foresay it. Howsoe'er,
  My brother hath done well.
BELARIUS   I had no mind
  To hunt this day. The boy Fidele's sickness
  Did make my way long forth.   149
GUIDERIUS   With his own sword,
  Which he did wave against my throat, I have ta'en   150
  His head from him. I'll throw't into the creek
  Behind our rock, and let it to the sea
  And tell the fishes he's the queen's son, Cloten.
  That's all I reck.   *Exit.*   154
BELARIUS   I fear 'twill be revenged.
  Would, Polydore, thou hadst not done't, though valor
  Becomes thee well enough.
ARVIRAGUS   Would I had done't,
  So the revenge alone pursued me. Polydore,   157
  I love thee brotherly, but envy much
  Thou hast robbed me of this deed. I would revenges
  That possible strength might meet would seek us through 160
  And put us to our answer.   161
BELARIUS   Well, 'tis done.
  We'll hunt no more today, nor seek for danger
  Where there's no profit. I prithee, to our rock;
  You and Fidele play the cooks. I'll stay
  Till hasty Polydore return, and bring him   165
  To dinner presently.
ARVIRAGUS   Poor sick Fidele,
  I'll willingly to him. To gain his color   167
  I'd let a parish of such Clotens blood   168
  And praise myself for charity.   *Exit.*

---

149 *Did . . . forth* made my walk forth (from the cave) seem long   154 *reck* care   157 *So* so that; *pursued* would have pursued   160 *possible* our available; *meet* i.e., in combat; *seek us through* come upon us   161 *put* force   165 *hasty* impetuous   167 *gain his color* restore the color (to) his (cheeks)   168 *let . . . blood* let blood for a parish of such Clotens (a medical term as a metaphor for "kill")

BELARIUS   O thou goddess,
170   Thou divine Nature, thou thyself thou blazon'st
       In these two princely boys! They are as gentle
       As zephyrs blowing below the violet,
       Not wagging his sweet head; and yet as rough,
174   Their royal blood enchafed, as the rud'st wind
       That by the top doth take the mountain pine
       And make him stoop to th' vale. 'Tis wonder
177   That an invisible instinct should frame them
178   To royalty unlearned, honor untaught,
179   Civility not seen from other, valor
180   That wildly grows in them but yields a crop
       As if it had been sowed. Yet still it's strange
       What Cloten's being here to us portends,
       Or what his death will bring us.
           Enter Guiderius.
GUIDERIUS   Where's my brother?
184   I have sent Cloten's clotpoll down the stream
       In embassy to his mother; his body's hostage
186   For his return.
           Solemn music.
BELARIUS   My ingenious instrument!
       Hark, Polydore, it sounds. But what occasion
188   Hath Cadwal now to give it motion? Hark!
GUIDERIUS
189   Is he at home?
BELARIUS   He went hence even now.
GUIDERIUS
190   What does he mean? Since death of my dear'st mother
       It did not speak before. All solemn things
192   Should answer solemn accidents. The matter?
193   Triumphs for nothing and lamenting toys

---

170 *blazon'st* depictest   174 *enchafed* heated   177 *frame* direct   178 *royalty*
kingly conduct   179 *Civility* civilized conduct   180 *wildly* spontaneously
184 *clotpoll* blockhead   186 *ingenious* skillfully constructed   188 *give it motion* play it   189 *even* just   192 *answer* correspond to; *accidents* events   193
lamenting toys lamenting for trifles

Is jollity for apes and grief for boys.
Is Cadwal mad?
    Enter Arviragus, with Imogen dead, bearing her in his
    arms.
BELARIUS   Look, here he comes,
And brings the dire occasion in his arms
Of what we blame him for.
ARVIRAGUS   The bird is dead
That we have made so much on. I had rather   198
Have skipped from sixteen years of age to sixty,
To have turned my leaping time into a crutch,   *200*
Than have seen this.
GUIDERIUS   O sweetest, fairest lily!
My brother wears thee not the one half so well
As when thou grew'st thyself.
BELARIUS   O melancholy,
Who ever yet could sound thy bottom, find   204
The ooze, to show what coast thy sluggish crare   205
Might eas'liest harbor in? Thou blessèd thing,   206
Jove knows what man thou mightst have made; but I,   207
Thou diedst, a most rare boy, of melancholy.
How found you him?   209
ARVIRAGUS   Stark, as you see,
Thus smiling, as some fly had tickled slumber,   210
Not as death's dart being laughed at; his right cheek   211
Reposing on a cushion.
GUIDERIUS   Where?
ARVIRAGUS   O' th' floor;
His arms thus leagued. I thought he slept, and put   213
My clouted brogues from off my feet, whose rudeness   214
Answered my steps too loud.

---

198 *on* of   204 *sound thy bottom* measure thy depths   205 *crare* small boat
206 *thing* i.e., Fidele   207 *but I* but I know that   209 *Stark* stiff (in rigor
mortis)   210 *as* as if   211 *as . . . at* as if the sting of death were being
laughed at   213 *leagued* crossed   214 *clouted brogues* hobnailed boots; *rude-*
ness coarseness (of the boots)

GUIDERIUS   Why, he but sleeps.
  If he be gone, he'll make his grave a bed;
  With female fairies will his tomb be haunted,
  And worms will not come to thee.
ARVIRAGUS   With fairest flowers,
  Whilst summer lasts and I live here, Fidele,
220 I'll sweeten thy sad grave. Thou shalt not lack
  The flower that's like thy face, pale primrose; nor
222 The azured harebell, like thy veins; no, nor
223 The leaf of eglantine, whom not to slander,
224 Outsweetened not thy breath. The ruddock would
  With charitable bill – O bill, sore shaming
  Those rich-left heirs that let their fathers lie
  Without a monument! – bring thee all this,
  Yea, and furred moss besides. When flowers are none
229 To winter-ground thy corpse –
GUIDERIUS   Prithee have done,
230 And do not play in wenchlike words with that
  Which is so serious. Let us bury him,
  And not protract with admiration what
233 Is now due debt. To th' grave.
ARVIRAGUS   Say, where shall's lay him?
GUIDERIUS
  By good Euriphile, our mother.
ARVIRAGUS   Be't so.
  And let us, Polydore, though now our voices
236 Have got the mannish crack, sing him to th' ground,
  As once to our mother; use like note and words,
  Save that Euriphile must be Fidele.
GUIDERIUS
  Cadwal,
240 I cannot sing. I'll weep, and word it with thee,

---

222 *azured* sky-blue   223 *eglantine* honeysuckle   224 *ruddock* robin (supposed to cover graves)   229 *To winter-ground* to protect in winter (some editors emend to "winter-gown")   230 *wenchlike* womanish   233 *shall's* shall
us (we)   236 *crack* break, tone   240 *word* speak, recite

For notes of sorrow out of tune are worse
Than priests and fanes that lie.   242
ARVIRAGUS   We'll speak it then.
BELARIUS
Great griefs, I see, med'cine the less, for Cloten
Is quite forgot. He was a queen's son, boys,
And though he came our enemy, remember
He was paid for that. Though mean and mighty, rotting   246
Together, have one dust, yet reverence,
That angel of the world, doth make distinction   248
Of place 'tween high and low. Our foe was princely,
And though you took his life as being our foe,   250
Yet bury him as a prince.
GUIDERIUS   Pray you fetch him hither.
Thersites' body is as good as Ajax'   252
When neither are alive.
ARVIRAGUS   If you'll go fetch him,
We'll say our song the whilst. Brother, begin.
                                    [Exit Belarius.]
GUIDERIUS
Nay, Cadwal, we must lay his head to th' east;   255
My father hath a reason for't.
ARVIRAGUS   'Tis true.
GUIDERIUS
Come on then and remove him.
ARVIRAGUS   So. Begin.

                    Song.

GUIDERIUS   Fear no more the heat o' th' sun
                 Nor the furious winter's rages;

---

242 *fanes* temples   246 *paid* punished   248 *angel . . . world* messenger sent
from heaven to earth   250 *as being* because he was   252 *Thersites* vindictive
and foul-mouthed Greek; *Ajax* Greek hero (though in Shakespeare's *Troilus
and Cressida* Ajax is distinctly unheroic)   255 *to th' east* (the opposite of
Christian practice; a way of suggesting the non-Christian world of the play)

260   Thou thy worldly task hast done,
       Home art gone and ta'en thy wages.
     Golden lads and girls all must,
263   As chimney sweepers, come to dust.

ARVIRAGUS Fear no more the frown o' th' great;
       Thou art past the tyrant's stroke.
     Care no more to clothe and eat;
       To thee the reed is as the oak.
268   The scepter, learning, physic, must
     All follow this and come to dust.

270 GUIDERIUS Fear no more the lightning flash,
271 ARVIRAGUS Nor th' all-dreaded thunderstone;
GUIDERIUS Fear not slander, censure rash;
ARVIRAGUS Thou hast finished joy and moan.
BOTH   All lovers young, all lovers must
275   Consign to thee and come to dust.

276 GUIDERIUS No exorciser harm thee,
ARVIRAGUS Nor no witchcraft charm thee.
278 GUIDERIUS Ghost unlaid forbear thee;
ARVIRAGUS Nothing ill come near thee.
280 BOTH   Quiet consummation have,
     And renownèd be thy grave.

  Enter Belarius with the body of Cloten.

GUIDERIUS
 We have done our obsequies. Come, lay him down.
BELARIUS
 Here's a few flowers, but 'bout midnight, more.
 The herbs that have on them cold dew o' th' night

---

263 *As* like **268** *scepter, learning, physic* kings, scholars, doctors **271** *thunderstone* thunderbolt **275** *Consign to thee* accept the same fate as you (some emend "thee" to "thou") **276** *exorciser* one who raises spirits **278** *unlaid* not driven out (by formal procedures); *forbear* leave alone **280** *consummation* fulfillment (i.e., death)

Are strewings fitt'st for graves. Upon their faces.   285
You were as flow'rs, now withered; even so   286
These herblets shall which we upon you strew.   287
Come on, away; apart upon our knees.   288
The ground that gave them first has them again.
Their pleasures here are past, so is their pain.   290
      Exeunt [Belarius, Guiderius, and Arviragus].
  Imogen awakes.
[IMOGEN]
Yes, sir, to Milford Haven. Which is the way?
I thank you. By yond bush? Pray, how far thither?
'Ods pittikins, can it be six mile yet?   293
I have gone all night. Faith, I'll lie down and sleep.   294
  [Sees the body of Cloten.]
But, soft, no bedfellow! O gods and goddesses!
These flow'rs are like the pleasures of the world;
This bloody man, the care on't. I hope I dream,
For so I thought I was a cave keeper   298
And cook to honest creatures. But 'tis not so;
'Twas but a bolt of nothing, shot at nothing,   300
Which the brain makes of fumes. Our very eyes   301
Are sometimes like our judgments, blind. Good faith,
I tremble still with fear, but if there be
Yet left in heaven as small a drop of pity
As a wren's eye, feared gods, a part of it!   305
The dream's here still. Even when I wake it is
Without me, as within me; not imagined, felt.
A headless man? The garments of Posthumus?

---

285 *Upon their faces* flowers on front of bodies (?), flowers lying face down (?)
(since Cloten's corpse has no head, it cannot mean that the corpses should be
placed face down) 286 *now* now you are 287 *shall* shall be (withered)
288 *apart . . . knees* we will pray elsewhere 293 *'Ods pittikins* God's little
pity (diminutive of "[I pray for] God's pity"; cf. ll. 304–5) 294 *gone* walked
298 *so* i.e., in a dream (such as this may be); *cave keeper* cave dweller 300
bolt arrow 301 *fumes* vapors believed to rise from the body to the brain and
cause dreams 305 *a part* i.e., grant me a part

I know the shape of's leg; this is his hand,
310   His foot Mercurial, his Martial thigh,
311   The brawns of Hercules; but his Jovial face –
      Murder in heaven? How? 'Tis gone. Pisanio,
313   All curses madded Hecuba gave the Greeks,
      And mine to boot, be darted on thee! Thou,
315   Conspired with that irregulous devil Cloten,
      Hath here cut off my lord. To write and read
      Be henceforth treacherous! Damned Pisanio
      Hath with his forgèd letters – damned Pisanio –
      From this most bravest vessel of the world
320   Struck the maintop. O Posthumus, alas,
      Where is thy head? Where's that? Ay me, where's that?
      Pisanio might have killed thee at the heart
      And left this head on. How should this be? Pisanio?
324   'Tis he and Cloten. Malice and lucre in them
325   Have laid this woe here. O, 'tis pregnant, pregnant!
      The drug he gave me, which he said was precious
327   And cordial to me, have I not found it
328   Murd'rous to th' senses? That confirms it home.
329   This is Pisanio's deed, and Cloten. O,
330   Give color to my pale cheek with thy blood,
      That we the horrider may seem to those
332   Which chance to find us. O my lord, my lord!
            [Falls on the body.]
            Enter Lucius, Captains, and a Soothsayer.

CAPTAIN
333   To them the legions garrisoned in Gallia
334   After your will have crossed the sea, attending

---

310 *Mercurial* quick, like Mercury's; *Martial* powerful, like Mars's 311 *brawns* muscles; *Jovial* like that of Jove, king of the gods 313 *madded* maddened; *Hecuba* wife of Priam, king of Troy: in some accounts, she went mad when Troy fell 315 *Conspired* conspiring; *irregulous* lawless 324 *lucre* greed 325 *pregnant* clear 327 *cordial* of medicinal value 328 *home* entirely (cf. "drives the point home") 329 *Cloten* (idiomatic for "Cloten's") 332 *Which* who 333 *To* besides; *them* i.e., forces mentioned by officers before coming onstage 334 *After* according to; *attending* waiting for

You here at Milford Haven with your ships.
They are here in readiness.
LUCIUS   But what from Rome?
CAPTAIN
  The Senate hath stirred up the confiners   337
  And gentlemen of Italy, most willing spirits
  That promise noble service, and they come
  Under the conduct of bold Iachimo,   340
  Siena's brother.   341
LUCIUS   When expect you them?
CAPTAIN
  With the next benefit o' th' wind.   342
LUCIUS   This forwardness
  Makes our hopes fair. Command our present numbers
  Be mustered; bid the captains look to't. Now, sir,
  What have you dreamed of late of this war's purpose? 345
SOOTHSAYER
  Last night the very gods showed me a vision –
  I fast and prayed for their intelligence – thus: 347
  I saw Jove's bird, the Roman eagle, winged
  From the spongy south to this part of the west,   349
  There vanished in the sunbeams; which portends,   350
  Unless my sins abuse my divination,   351
  Success to th' Roman host.
LUCIUS   Dream often so,
  And never false. Soft, ho, what trunk is here?   353
  Without his top? The ruin speaks that sometime
  It was a worthy building. How, a page?
  Or dead or sleeping on him? But dead rather,   356
  For nature doth abhor to make his bed   357

---

337 *confiners* inhabitants   341 *Siena's* Duke of Siena's   342 *forwardness*
moving ahead (on schedule)   345 *of late* lately; *this war's purpose* our achiev-
ing our purpose in this war   347 *fast* fasted; *their intelligence* information
from them   349 *spongy* damp   351 *abuse* mislead   353 *false* (dream) falsely
356 *Or* either   357 *nature doth abhor* man naturally abhors

358   With the defunct or sleep upon the dead.
        Let's see the boy's face.
        CAPTAIN   He's alive, my lord.
        LUCIUS
360   He'll, then, instruct us of this body. Young one,
        Inform us of thy fortunes, for it seems
362   They crave to be demanded. Who is this
        Thou mak'st thy bloody pillow? Or who was he
364   That, otherwise than noble nature did,
        Hath altered that good picture? What's thy interest
366   In this sad wreck? How came't? Who is't? What art
          thou?
        IMOGEN
          I am nothing, or if not,
        Nothing to be were better. This was my master,
        A very valiant Briton and a good,
370   That here by mountaineers lies slain. Alas,
        There is no more such masters. I may wander
        From east to occident, cry out for service,
        Try many, all good, serve truly, never
        Find such another master.
        LUCIUS   'Lack, good youth
375   Thou mov'st no less with thy complaining than
        Thy master in bleeding. Say his name, good friend.
        IMOGEN
          Richard du Champ. *[Aside]* If I do lie and do
        No harm by it, though the gods hear, I hope
        They'll pardon it. Say you, sir?
        LUCIUS   Thy name?
        IMOGEN   Fidele, sir.
        LUCIUS
380   Thou dost approve thyself the very same;

        _____

        358 *defunct* dead   360 *instruct us of* inform us about   362 *crave . . . de-*
        manded beg to be asked about (i.e., are such as to arouse curiosity or sympa-
        thy)   364 *otherwise . . . did* from the form given it by noble nature   366
        wreck ruin   375 *mov'st no less* art no less moving   380 *approve* prove (be-
        cause "Fidele" means "faithful")

Thy name well fits thy faith, thy faith thy name.
Wilt take thy chance with me? I will not say
Thou shalt be so well mastered, but be sure
No less beloved. The Roman emperor's letters
Sent by a consul to me should not sooner
Than thine own worth prefer thee. Go with me.   386

IMOGEN
I'll follow, sir. But first, an't please the gods,   387
I'll hide my master from the flies, as deep
As these poor pickaxes can dig; and when   389
With wild wood-leaves and weeds I ha' strewed his grave   *390*
And on it said a century of prayers,   391
Such as I can, twice o'er, I'll weep and sigh,   392
And leaving so his service, follow you,
So please you entertain me.   394

LUCIUS   Ay, good youth,
And rather father thee than master thee.
My friends,
The boy hath taught us manly duties. Let us
Find out the prettiest daisied plot we can
And make him with our pikes and partisans   399
A grave. Come, arm him. Boy, he's preferred   400
By thee to us, and he shall be interred
As soldiers can. Be cheerful; wipe thine eyes.
Some falls are means the happier to arise.   *Exeunt.*

*

❧ **IV.3** *Enter Cymbeline, Lords, and Pisanio.*

CYMBELINE
Again, and bring me word how 'tis with her.

[Exit a Lord.]

---

386 *prefer* recommend   387 *an't* if it   389 *pickaxes* i.e., fingers 391 ᴜᴘᴴ
tury hundred   392 *can* know   394 *So* if it; *entertain* employ 3 ᴾᴴ *artisans*
long-handled weapons   400 *arm him* carry him in your ʜɴɪɪs; *preferred* rec-
ommended
  IV.3 Cymbeline's palace

A fever with the absence of her son,
A madness, of which her life's in danger. Heavens,
4   How deeply you at once do touch me! Imogen,
The great part of my comfort, gone; my queen
6   Upon a desperate bed, and in a time
When fearful wars point at me; her son gone,
8   So needful for this present. It strikes me past
The hope of comfort. But for thee, fellow,
10   Who needs must know of her departure and
11   Dost seem so ignorant, we'll enforce it from thee
By a sharp torture.

PISANIO   Sir, my life is yours,
I humbly set it at your will; but for my mistress,
I nothing know where she remains, why gone,
Nor when she purposes return. Beseech your highness,
16   Hold me your loyal servant.

LORD   Good my liege,
The day that she was missing he was here.
I dare be bound he's true and shall perform
19   All parts of his subjection loyally. For Cloten,
20   There wants no diligence in seeking him,
21   And will no doubt be found.

CYMBELINE   The time is troublesome.
    [To Pisanio]
22   We'll slip you for a season, but our jealousy
23   Does yet depend.

LORD   So please your majesty,
The Roman legions, all from Gallia drawn,
Are landed on your coast, with a supply
Of Roman gentlemen by the Senate sent.

---

4 *touch* wound 6 *desperate* i.e., she is critically ill 8 *needful* needed; *It . . . past* the blow to me is beyond 11 *enforce . . . thee* force you to talk, get it out of you 16 *Hold* consider 19 *subjection* duties as a subject 21 *will* he will; *troublesome* full of troubles, seriously disturbed 22 *slip* turn loose; *jealousy* suspicion 23 *depend* hang (over you)

CYMBELINE
    Now for the counsel of my son and queen!   27
    I am amazed with matter.   28
LORD   Good my liege,
    Your preparation can affront no less   29
    Than what you hear of. Come more, for more you're 30
       ready.
    The want is but to put those pow'rs in motion   31
    That long to move.
CYMBELINE   I thank you. Let's withdraw,
    And meet the time as it seeks us. We fear not
    What can from Italy annoy us, but   34
    We grieve at chances here. Away.
                             Exeunt [all but Pisanio].

PISANIO
    I heard no letter from my master since   36
    I wrote him Imogen was slain. 'Tis strange.
    Nor hear I from my mistress, who did promise
    To yield me often tidings. Neither know I
    What is betid to Cloten, but remain   40
    Perplexed in all. The heavens still must work.
    Wherein I am false I am honest; not true, to be true.
    These present wars shall find I love my country,
    Even to the note o' th' king, or I'll fall in them.   44
    All other doubts, by time let them be cleared;
    Fortune brings in some boats that are not steered. *Exit.*

                        *

27 *Now for* if only I now had   28 *amazed with matter* confused by (all the) business   29 *preparation* armed force; *affront* confront   29–30 *no less / Than* an army as large as   30 *Come more* if more come   31 *The . . . but* all that's needed is   34 *annoy* injure   36 *no letter* not a whit   40 *betid* happened   44 *note o'* recognition by

∾ **IV.4** *Enter Belarius, Guiderius, and Arviragus.*

GUIDERIUS
    The noise is round about us.
BELARIUS   Let us from it.
ARVIRAGUS
2   What pleasure, sir, find we in life, to lock it
    From action and adventure?
GUIDERIUS   Nay, what hope
4   Have we in hiding us? This way the Romans
5   Must or for Britons slay us or receive us
    For barbarous and unnatural revolts
    During their use, and slay us after.
BELARIUS   Sons,
8   We'll higher to the mountains, there secure us.
    To the king's party there's no going. Newness
10   Of Cloten's death – we being not known, not mustered
11   Among the bands – may drive us to a render
    Where we have lived, and so extort from's that
13   Which we have done, whose answer would be death
14   Drawn on with torture.
GUIDERIUS   This is, sir, a doubt
    In such a time nothing becoming you
    Nor satisfying us.
ARVIRAGUS   It is not likely
    That when they hear the Roman horses neigh,
18   Behold their quartered fires, have both their eyes
19   And ears so cloyed importantly as now,

IV.4 Wales   2 *to lock it* when it is closed off   4 *This way* i.e., if we hide   5 *Must or* must either   5–7 *receive . . . use* i.e., accept us as savage and un-natural rebels and use us for a time against the British   8 *secure us* make our-selves safe   10 *mustered* enrolled   11 *render* account   13 *whose answer* to which the reply (i.e., the penalty)   14 *Drawn on with* led up to by   18 *quartered* camp; *fires* (some editors emend to "files" to suggest imminent at-tack)   19 *cloyed importantly* filled with important business

That they will waste their time upon our note,   20
To know from whence we are.
BELARIUS   O, I am known
Of many in the army. Many years,
Though Cloten then but young, you see, not wore him   23
From my remembrance. And besides, the king
Hath not deserved my service nor your loves,   25
Who find in my exile the want of breeding,
The certainty of this hard life; aye hopeless   27
To have the courtesy your cradle promised,   28
But to be still hot summer's tanlings and   29
The shrinking slaves of winter.   30
GUIDERIUS   Than be so
Better to cease to be. Pray, sir, to th' army.
I and my brother are not known; yourself
So out of thought, and thereto so o'ergrown,   33
Cannot be questioned.   34
ARVIRAGUS   By this sun that shines,
I'll thither. What thing is't that I never
Did see man die, scarce ever looked on blood
But that of coward hares, hot goats, and venison,   37
Never bestrid a horse, save one that had
A rider like myself, who ne'er wore rowel   39
Nor iron on his heel! I am ashamed   40
To look upon the holy sun, to have
The benefit of his blessed beams, remaining
So long a poor unknown.
GUIDERIUS   By heavens, I'll go.
If you will bless me, sir, and give me leave,

---

20 *upon our note* in noticing us **23** *then* was then; *not wore* did not wear
(i.e., erase) **25–26** *your ... breeding* the love of you two who because of my
exile meet with lack of cultivation **27** *certainty* inescapability **27–28** *aye
hopeless ... courtesy* ever without hope of having the courtly style **28** *cradle*
birth **29** *tanlings* tanned persons – i.e., living in the open, unsheltered **33**
o'ergrown bearded (?), grown old (?) **34** *questioned* i.e., on your identity **37**
hot lecherous **39–40** *ne'er ... heel* i.e., never had standard riding equipment

I'll take the better care, but if you will not,
46   The hazard therefore due fall on me by
     The hands of Romans!
ARVIRAGUS   So say I. Amen.
BELARIUS
48   No reason I, since of your lives you set
     So slight a valuation, should reserve
50   My cracked one to more care. Have with you, boys!
51   If in your country wars you chance to die,
     That is my bed too, lads, and there I'll lie.
     Lead, lead. *[Aside]* The time seems long; their blood
        thinks scorn
     Till it fly out and show them princes born.   *Exeunt.*

                          *

∽ **V.1** *Enter Posthumus alone [with a bloody*
   handkerchief].

POSTHUMUS
     Yea, bloody cloth, I'll keep thee, for I wished
     Thou shouldst be colored thus. You married ones,
3 · If each of you should take this course, how many
     Must murder wives much better than themselves
5   For wrying but a little! O Pisanio,
6   Every good servant does not all commands;
7   No bond but to do just ones. Gods, if you
     Should have ta'en vengeance on my faults, I never
9   Had lived to put on this; so had you saved
10   The noble Imogen to repent, and struck
     Me, wretch more worth your vengeance. But alack,

---

46 *hazard ... due* danger arising from being unblessed   48 *of* on   50
cracked i.e., with age   51 *country* country's
     V.1 s.d. (Posthumus is dressed as an Italian gentleman; see V.1.23)   3
take this course do as I have done   5 *wrying* erring   6 *does not* does not
carry out   7 *No bond but* he is bound only   9 *put on* instigate (?), load myself with (?)   10 *repent* i.e., for the misdeeds he imputes to her

You snatch some hence for little faults; that's love,
To have them fall no more; you some permit   13
To second ills with ills, each elder worse,   14
And make them dread it, to the doers' thrift.   15
But Imogen is your own. Do your best wills,   16
And make me blessed to obey. I am brought hither
Among th' Italian gentry, and to fight
Against my lady's kingdom. 'Tis enough
That, Britain, I have killed thy mistress; peace,   20
I'll give no wound to thee. Therefore, good heavens,
Hear patiently my purpose. I'll disrobe me
Of these Italian weeds and suit myself   23
As does a Briton peasant. So I'll fight
Against the part I come with; so I'll die   25
For thee, O Imogen, even for whom my life
Is every breath a death; and thus, unknown,
Pitied nor hated, to the face of peril
Myself I'll dedicate. Let me make men know
More valor in me than my habits show.   30
Gods, put the strength o' th' Leonati in me.
To shame the guise o' th' world, I will begin   32
The fashion, less without and more within.   33

                                        Exit.

                        ∗

∾ **V.2** *Enter Lucius, Iachimo, and the Roman Army at*
one door, and the Briton Army at another, Leonatus
Posthumus following like a poor soldier. They march
over and go out. Then enter again in skirmish Iachimo

---

13 *fall* i.e., into faults 14 *second* duplicate, back up; *elder* i.e., later (as if
evils were becoming more "mature" with time) 15 *them* i.e., the doers;
dread it repent the evil course; *thrift* profit, gain 16 *best* (often emended to
"blest") 20 *mistress; peace* (has been emended to "mistress-piece," a rare but
existing version of "master-piece") 23 *weeds* clothes; *suit* dress 25 *part* side
30 *habits show* clothes proclaim 32 *guise* habit 33 *fashion, less without* i.e.,
fashion of having less external show

and Posthumus. He vanquisheth and disarmeth
Iachimo and then leaves him.

IACHIMO
   The heaviness and guilt within my bosom
2 Takes off my manhood. I have belied a lady,
3 The princess of this country, and the air on't
4 Revengingly enfeebles me; or could this carl,
   A very drudge of nature's, have subdued me
   In my profession? Knighthoods and honors, borne
   As I wear mine, are titles but of scorn.
8 If that thy gentry, Britain, go before
   This lout as he exceeds our lords, the odds
10 Is that we scarce are men and you are gods.   *Exit.*
      The battle continues. The Britons fly; Cymbeline is
      taken. Then enter, to his rescue, Belarius, Guiderius,
      and Arviragus.

BELARIUS
   Stand, stand! We have th' advantage of the ground.
   The lane is guarded. Nothing routs us but
   The villainy of our fears.
GUIDERIUS, ARVIRAGUS   Stand, stand, and fight!
      Enter Posthumus, and seconds the Britons. They rescue
      Cymbeline and exeunt. Then enter Lucius, Iachimo,
      and Imogen.

LUCIUS
   Away, boy, from the troops, and save thyself,
   For friends kill friends, and the disorder's such
16 As war were hoodwinked.
IACHIMO   'Tis their fresh supplies.
LUCIUS
17 It is a day turned strangely; or betimes
   Let's reinforce or fly.   *Exeunt.*

V.2   2 *off* away   3 *on't* of it   4 *or* otherwise; *carl* peasant   8 *go before* excel
16 *hoodwinked* blindfolded   17 *or* either; *betimes* in time

*

∾ **V.3** *Enter Posthumus and a Briton Lord.*

LORD
   Cam'st thou from where they made the stand?
POSTHUMUS   I did;
   Though you, it seems, come from the fliers.
LORD   I did.
POSTHUMUS
   No blame be to you, sir, for all was lost,
   But that the heavens fought. The king himself
   Of his wings destitute, the army broken,
   And but the backs of Britons seen, all flying
   Through a strait lane; the enemy fullhearted,   7
   Lolling the tongue with slaught'ring, having work   8
   More plentiful than tools to do't, struck down
   Some mortally, some slightly touched, some falling   10
   Merely through fear, that the strait pass was dammed
   With dead men hurt behind, and cowards living   12
   To die with lengthened shame.
LORD   Where was this lane?
POSTHUMUS
   Close by the battle, ditched, and walled with turf;
   Which gave advantage to an ancient soldier,
   An honest one I warrant, who deserved   16
   So long a breeding as his white beard came to,
   In doing this for's country. Athwart the lane
   He with two striplings – lads more like to run   19

V.3 s.d. (Posthumus is still dressed as a "Briton peasant"; cf. V.1.24) **7** *strait*
narrow; *full-hearted* with high morale **8** *Lolling the tongue* letting their
tongues hang out (like wild animals) **10** *touched* wounded **12** *behind* i.e.,
while running away **16–17** *deserved . . . to* (1) deserved to live so long as to
breed this long white beard, (2) deserved to be cherished in the future for as
long as his white beard showed he had already lived **19–20** *run . . . base*
play the children's game of prisoner's base

20 The country base than to commit such slaughter;
21 With faces fit for masks, or rather fairer
22 Than those for preservation cased or shame –
    Made good the passage, cried to those that fled,
    "Our Britain's harts die flying, not our men.
25 To darkness fleet souls that fly backwards. Stand,
26 Or we are Romans and will give you that
27 Like beasts which you shun beastly, and may save
    But to look back in frown. Stand, stand!" These three,
    Three thousand confident, in act as many –
30 For three performers are the file when all
    The rest do nothing – with this word "Stand, stand,"
32 Accommodated by the place, more charming
    With their own nobleness, which could have turned
34 A distaff to a lance, gilded pale looks,
35 Part shame, part spirit renewed; that some, turned
      coward
36 But by example – O, a sin in war,
37 Damned in the first beginners! – gan to look
38 The way that they did and to grin like lions
    Upon the pikes o' th' hunters. Then began
40 A stop i' th' chaser, a retire; anon
    A rout, confusion thick. Forthwith they fly
42 Chickens the way which they stooped eagles; slaves,
43 The strides they victors made; and now our cowards,

---

21 *fit for masks* delicate enough to justify protection against the sun   22
those for . . . shame those (ladies'?) faces covered for such protection or for
modesty   25 *fleet* hurry   26 *we are Romans* we shall play the part of Romans
27–28 *save . . . frown* prevent by looking back fiercely   27 *beastly* i.e., like
cowards   30 *file* whole force   32 *Accommodated* given an advantage; *more
charming* spellbinding   34 *A distaff . . . lance* a housewife into a soldier;
gilded restored color to   35 *Part . . . part* in some . . . in others   36 *by example* by imitating others   37 *gan* began   37–38 *look / The way* face in the
direction   38 *they* i.e., Belarius and his sons; *grin* i.e., bare the teeth   40
chaser pursuer; *retire* retreat   42 *Chickens* like chickens; *way* route; *stooped
eagles* swooped over like eagles; *slaves* like slaves (they fly back over)   43 *victors* as victors

Like fragments in hard voyages, became   44
The life o' th' need. Having found the back door open   45
Of the unguarded hearts, heavens, how they wound!
Some slain before, some dying, some their friends   47
O'erborne i' th' former wave, ten chased by one
Are now each one the slaughterman of twenty.
Those that would die or ere resist are grown   50
The mortal bugs o' th' field.   51
LORD   This was strange chance:
A narrow lane, an old man, and two boys.
POSTHUMUS
Nay, do not wonder at it. You are made
Rather to wonder at the things you hear
Than to work any. Will you rhyme upon't   55
And vent it for a mock'ry? Here is one: 56
"Two boys, an old man twice a boy, a lane,
Preserved the Britons, was the Romans' bane."
LORD
Nay, be not angry, sir.   59
POSTHUMUS   'Lack, to what end?
Who dares not stand his foe, I'll be his friend;   60
For if he'll do as he is made to do,   61
I know he'll quickly fly my friendship too.
You have put me into rhyme.   63
LORD   Farewell. You're angry. *Exit.*
POSTHUMUS
Still going? This is a lord! O noble misery,   64
To be i' th' field, and ask "What news?" of me!

---

44 *fragments* i.e., of food   45 *life . . . need* support of life in time of need
45–46 *Having . . . hearts* i.e., having found that the Romans were not invul-
nerable   47 *slain* i.e., having played dead; *dying* severely wounded; *their
friends* friends of those already mentioned   50 *or ere* rather than   51 *mortal
bugs* deadly terrors (cf. "bugbears")   55 *work any* perform such (things)   56
vent it air it, let it get around   59 *'Lack* alack, alas   60 *stand* withstand   61
as . . . do as it is natural for him to do   63 *put . . . rhyme* made me versify
64 *going* running away; *noble misery* wretch of a noble

Today how many would have given their honors
To have saved their carcasses, took heel to do't,
68   And yet died too! I, in mine own woe charmed,
Could not find Death where I did hear him groan
70   Nor feel him where he struck. Being an ugly monster,
71   'Tis strange he hides him in fresh cups, soft beds,
Sweet words, or hath more ministers than we
That draw his knives i' th' war. Well, I will find him,
74   For being now a favorer to the Briton,
75   No more a Briton. I have resumed again
76   The part I came in. Fight I will no more,
77   But yield me to the veriest hind that shall
78   Once touch my shoulder. Great the slaughter is
79   Here made by th' Roman; great the answer be
80   Britons must take. For me, my ransom's death.
81   On either side I come to spend my breath,
Which neither here I'll keep nor bear again,
But end it by some means for Imogen.
       Enter two [Briton] Captains and Soldiers.
FIRST CAPTAIN
   Great Jupiter be praised, Lucius is taken.
   'Tis thought the old man and his sons were angels.
SECOND CAPTAIN
86   There was a fourth man, in a silly habit,
87   That gave th' affront with them.
FIRST CAPTAIN   So 'tis reported,
   But none of 'em can be found. Stand, who's there?
POSTHUMUS
   A Roman,

---

68 *charmed* i.e., "leading a charmed life"   71–72 *hides . . . words* i.e., appears from unexpected places   74 *being . . . favorer* death now favoring   75 *No more* I will no more be   76 *part . . . in* i.e., his role as a Roman (as the way to find death, now helping the British by taking their enemies; the line suggests that Posthumus puts back on the costume he was wearing as an Italian gentleman in V.1)   77 *hind* peasant   78 *touch my shoulder* i.e., as sign of arrest   79 *answer* retaliation   81 *spend my breath* yield my life   86 *silly habit* simple garb   87 *affront* attack

Who had not now been drooping here if seconds   90
Had answered him.   91
SECOND CAPTAIN   Lay hands on him. A dog,
A leg of Rome shall not return to tell
What crows have pecked them here. He brags his service
As if he were of note. Bring him to th' king.   94
   Enter Cymbeline, Belarius, Guiderius, Arviragus,
   Pisanio, and Roman Captives. The Captains present
   Posthumus to Cymbeline, who delivers him over to a
   Jailer.   *[Exeunt.]*

                    *

～ **V.4** *Enter Posthumus and [two] Jailer[s].*

FIRST JAILER
You shall not now be stol'n; you have locks upon you.
So graze as you find pasture.
SECOND JAILER   Ay, or a stomach.
                    [Exeunt Jailers.]
POSTHUMUS
Most welcome, bondage, for thou art a way,
I think, to liberty. Yet am I better
Than one that's sick o' th' gout, since he had rather
Groan so in perpetuity than be cured
By th' sure physician, Death, who is the key
T' unbar these locks. My conscience, thou art fettered
More than my shanks and wrists. You good gods, give me
The penitent instrument to pick that bolt,   10
Then free for ever. Is't enough I am sorry?   11
So children temporal fathers do appease;   12

---

90 *seconds* supporters 91 *answered him* acted as he did 94 s.d. *Exeunt* (It is
usual to mark a new scene at this point, following F, but an exit and immediate reentrance for Posthumus and his jailer(s) would be extremely unusual
in Shakespeare. It is more likely that they would stay onstage at this point
while everyone else leaves.)
   V.4 **10** *penitent . . . bolt* penitence to unfetter my conscience **11** *free*
i.e., in death **12** *So* i.e., by being sorry

Gods are more full of mercy. Must I repent,
14 I cannot do it better than in gyves,
15 Desired more than constrained. To satisfy,
16 If of my freedom 'tis the main part, take
17 No stricter render of me than my all.
I know you are more clement than vile men,
Who of their broken debtors take a third,
20 A sixth, a tenth, letting them thrive again
21 On their abatement. That's not my desire.
For Imogen's dear life take mine; and though
'Tis not so dear, yet 'tis a life; you coined it.
24 'Tween man and man they weigh not every stamp;
25 Though light, take pieces for the figure's sake;
26 You rather mine, being yours. And so, great pow'rs,
27 If you will take this audit, take this life
28 And cancel these cold bonds. O Imogen,
I'll speak to thee in silence.
    [Sleeps.]

*Solemn music. Enter, as in an apparition, Sicilius
Leonatus, father to Posthumus, an old man attired like
a warrior, leading in his hand an ancient Matron, his
wife and mother to Posthumus, with music before
them. Then, after other music, follow the two young
Leonati, brothers to Posthumus, with wounds as they
died in the wars. They circle Posthumus round as he
lies sleeping.*

---

14 *gyves* fetters   15 *constrained* forced upon me; *satisfy* atone   16 *If . . . part*
if it (atonement) is essential to my freedom (of conscience)   17 *stricter render* sterner repayment; *all* i.e., life   21 *abatement* reduced principal; *That's*
i.e., to thrive again   24 *'Tween man and man* in business dealings between
men; *stamp* coin (to check that it is not underweight)   25 *figure's* i.e., of the
royal image on the coin   26 *You . . . yours* you more readily take my life
(light coin though it is) because you made it   27 *take* accept   28 *cold* heavy,
depressing; *bonds* (1) contract for his life, (2) prison fetters

SICILIUS	No more, thou thunder master, show	30
	Thy spite on mortal flies.	
	With Mars fall out, with Juno chide,	
	That thy adulteries	33
	Rates and revenges.	34
	Hath my poor boy done aught but well,	
	Whose face I never saw?	
	I died whilst in the womb he stayed	
	Attending nature's law;	38
	Whose father then, as men report	
	Thou orphans' father art,	40
	Thou shouldst have been, and shielded him	
	From this earth-vexing smart.	42
MOTHER	Lucina lent not me her aid,	43
	But took me in my throes,	
	That from me was Posthumus ripped,	
	Came crying 'mongst his foes,	
	A thing of pity.	
SICILIUS	Great Nature like his ancestry	
	Molded the stuff so fair	49
	That he deserved the praise o' th' world,	50
	As great Sicilius' heir.	
1st BROTHER	When once he was mature for man,	52
	In Britain where was he	
	That could stand up his parallel,	
	Or fruitful object be	
	In eye of Imogen, that best	
	Could deem his dignity?	57
MOTHER	With marriage wherefore was he mocked,	

---

30 *thunder master* Jupiter   **33** *That* who   **34** *Rates* scolds   **38** *Attending nature's law* awaiting the completion of the natural process   **42** *earth-vexing smart* suffering that afflicts earthly life   **43** *Lucina* goddess of childbirth   **49** *stuff* substance (cf. I.1.23)   **52** *mature for man* grown up   **57** *deem his dignity* judge his worth

		To be exiled and thrown
60		From Leonati seat and cast
		From her his dearest one,
		Sweet Imogen?

63	SICILIUS	Why did you suffer Iachimo,
64		Slight thing of Italy,
65		To taint his nobler heart and brain
		With needless jealousy,
67		And to become the geck and scorn
		O' th' other's villainy?

69	2d BROTHER	For this from stiller seats we came,
70		Our parents and us twain,
71		That striking in our country's cause
		Fell bravely and were slain,
73		Our fealty and Tenantius' right
		With honor to maintain.

75	1st BROTHER	Like hardiment Posthumus hath
		To Cymbeline performed.
		Then, Jupiter, thou king of gods,
78		Why hast thou thus adjourned
		The graces for his merits due,
80		Being all to dolors turned?

	SICILIUS	Thy crystal window ope; look out.
		No longer exercise
		Upon a valiant race thy harsh
		And potent injuries.

| | MOTHER | Since, Jupiter, our son is good, |
| 86 | | Take off his miseries. |

| | SICILIUS | Peep through thy marble mansion. Help, |

---

63 *suffer* allow   64 *Slight* contemptible   65 *taint* infect   67 *geck* dupe   69 *stiller seats* quieter dwelling places (Elysium)   71 *That* who   73 *Tenantius* Cymbeline's father   75 *hardiment* courageous deeds   78 *adjourned* put off   80 *dolors* sorrows   86 *off* away

                    Or we poor ghosts will cry
                    To th' shining synod of the rest   89
                    Against thy deity.   90

BROTHERS   Help, Jupiter, or we appeal
                    And from thy justice fly.

*Jupiter descends in thunder and lightning, sitting upon
an eagle. He throws a thunderbolt. The Ghosts fall on
their knees.*

JUPITER
  No more, you petty spirits of region low,
        Offend our hearing. Hush! How dare you ghosts
  Accuse the thunderer, whose bolt, you know,
        Sky-planted, batters all rebelling coasts?   96
  Poor shadows of Elysium, hence, and rest
        Upon your never-withering banks of flow'rs.
  Be not with mortal accidents opprest.   99
        No care of yours it is; you know 'tis ours.   100
  Whom best I love I cross; to make my gift,
        The more delayed, delighted. Be content.   102
  Your low-laid son our godhead will uplift;
        His comforts thrive, his trials well are spent.   104
  Our Jovial star reigned at his birth, and in   105
        Our temple was he married. Rise, and fade.
  He shall be lord of Lady Imogen,
        And happier much by his affliction made.
  This tablet lay upon his breast, wherein
        Our pleasure his full fortune doth confine.   110
  *[He gives them a tablet, which they lay on Posthumus's
  breast.]*

---

89 *synod . . . rest* assembly of the gods   **96** *Sky-planted* growing in the sky,
based in the sky   **99** *accidents* events   **102** *delighted* (the more) delighted in
104 *spent* ended   **105** *Jovial star* planet Jupiter, supposed to bring good fortune   **110** *confine* set down concisely

And so, away; no farther with your din
Express impatience, lest you stir up mine.
Mount, eagle, to my palace crystalline.   *Ascends.*

SICILIUS
He came in thunder; his celestial breath
Was sulphurous to smell; the holy eagle
116 Stooped, as to foot us. His ascension is
117 More sweet than our blessed fields; his royal bird
Preens the immortal wing and claws his beak,
As when his god is pleased.
ALL   Thanks, Jupiter.
SICILIUS
120 The marble pavement closes; he is entered
His radiant roof. Away, and, to be blest,
Let us with care perform his great behest.
                                    [The Ghosts] vanish.

POSTHUMUS *[Waking]*
Sleep, thou hast been a grandsire and begot
A father to me, and thou hast created
125 A mother and two brothers; but, O scorn,
Gone! They went hence so soon as they were born.
And so I am awake. Poor wretches that depend
On greatness' favor dream as I have done,
129 Wake, and find nothing. But, alas, I swerve.
130 Many dream not to find, neither deserve,
And yet are steeped in favors. So am I,
That have this golden chance and know not why.
133 What fairies haunt this ground? A book? O rare one,
134 Be not, as is our fangled world, a garment
Nobler than that it covers. Let thy effects

------

116 *Stooped . . . foot* swooped as if to seize (with claws)   117 *More sweet* i.e.,
in contrast with the sulphurous descent   120 *marble pavement* i.e., heaven
125 *O scorn* what a bitter joke   129 *swerve* err (cf. "I'm off the track")   133
book i.e., the tablet of l. 109   134 *fangled* dressy, fancy

So follow to be most unlike our courtiers,   136
As good as promise.
Reads.

"When as a lion's whelp shall, to himself unknown,   138
without seeking find, and be embraced by a piece of   139
tender air; and when from a stately cedar shall be lopped *140*
branches which, being dead many years, shall after
revive, be jointed to the old stock, and freshly grow;
then shall Posthumus end his miseries, Britain be fortu-
nate and flourish in peace and plenty."
'Tis still a dream, or else such stuff as madmen
Tongue, and brain not; either both, or nothing,   146
Or senseless speaking, or a speaking such   147
As sense cannot untie. Be what it is,
The action of my life is like it, which   149
I'll keep, if but for sympathy.   150
Enter Jailer.

JAILER   Come, sir, are you ready for death?
POSTHUMUS   Overroasted rather; ready long ago.
JAILER   Hanging is the word, sir. If you be ready for that, 153
you are well cooked.
POSTHUMUS   So, if I prove a good repast to the spectators, the dish pays the shot.   156
JAILER   A heavy reckoning for you, sir. But the comfort
is, you shall be called to no more payments, fear no
more tavern bills, which are often the sadness of part- 159
ing, as the procuring of mirth. You come in faint for   *160*
want of meat, depart reeling with too much drink;
sorry that you have paid too much, and sorry that you
are paid too much; purse and brain both empty; the   163

---

136 *to* as to   138 *When as* when   139 *piece* creature, morsel   146 *Tongue*
say; *brain* understand   147 *senseless* irrational   147–48 *such . . . untie* too
cryptic for rational analysis   149 *like it* i.e., in being difficult to understand
150 *sympathy* resemblance   153 *Hanging* (pun on death by hanging and
hanging up of meat)   156 *dish* food; *shot* reckoning   159 *often* as often
163 *are paid* are paid off, punished (by too much liquor)

brain the heavier for being too light, the purse too
165   light, being drawn of heaviness. O, of this contradiction you shall now be quit. O, the charity of a penny
167   cord! It sums up thousands in a trice. You have no true
168   debitor and creditor but it; of what's past, is, and to
169   come, the discharge. Your neck, sir, is pen, book, and
170   counters; so the acquittance follows.
171   POSTHUMUS   I am merrier to die than thou art to live.

JAILER   Indeed, sir, he that sleeps feels not the toothache;
173   but a man that were to sleep your sleep, and a hangman
to help him to bed, I think he would change places
175   with his officer; for look you, sir, you know not which
way you shall go.
POSTHUMUS   Yes indeed do I, fellow.

JAILER   Your death has eyes in's head then. I have not seen
179   him so pictured. You must either be directed by some
180   that take upon them to know, or to take upon yourself
181   that which I am sure you do not know, or jump the
182   after-inquiry on your own peril. And how you shall
183   speed in your journey's end, I think you'll never return
to tell one.

POSTHUMUS   I tell thee, fellow, there are none want eyes
186   to direct them the way I am going but such as wink and
will not use them.

188   JAILER   What an infinite mock is this, that a man should
have the best use of eyes to see the way of blindness! I
190   am sure hanging's the way of winking.
            Enter a Messenger.

---

165 *drawn* emptied   167 *cord* i.e., for hanging   168 *debitor and creditor* accountant   169 *discharge* payment   170 *counters* round pieces of metal used
for reckoning; *acquittance* receipt   171 *to die . . . to live* in dying . . . in living   173 *a man that were* as for a man scheduled   175 *officer* i.e., the hangman   179 *so pictured* i.e., in the conventional skull representing death;
some clergy (?)   180 *take upon yourself* decide for yourself (on your salvation)
181 *jump* gamble on   182 *after-inquiry* final judgment   183 *speed in* make
out at   186 *wink* close   188 *mock* joke

MESSENGER   Knock off his manacles; bring your prisoner
to the king.

POSTHUMUS   Thou bring'st good news; I am called to be
made free.   194

JAILER   I'll be hanged then.

POSTHUMUS   Thou shalt be then freer than a jailer. No
bolts for the dead.   *Exeunt [Posthumus and Messenger].*

JAILER   Unless a man would marry a gallows and beget
young gibbets, I never saw one so prone. Yet, on my   199
conscience, there are verier knaves desire to live, for all   *200*
he be a Roman; and there be some of them too that die   201
against their wills. So should I, if I were one. I would
we were all of one mind, and one mind good. O, there
were desolation of jailers and gallowses! I speak against
my present profit, but my wish hath a preferment in't.   205
                                                    [Exit.]

                            *

∾ **V.5** *Enter Cymbeline, Belarius, Guiderius, Arviragus,*
Pisanio, and Lords.

CYMBELINE
Stand by my side, you whom the gods have made
Preservers of my throne. Woe is my heart
That the poor soldier that so richly fought,
Whose rags shamed gilded arms, whose naked breast
Stepped before targes of proof, cannot be found.   5
He shall be happy that can find him, if
Our grace can make him so.   7
BELARIUS   I never saw
Such noble fury in so poor a thing,

---

194 *made free* i.e., by death   199 *prone* inclined (to die)   201–2 *and there*
be . . . wills (Romans were usually thought of as Stoics and therefore indiffer-
ent to death)   205 *hath . . . in't* includes a better position for myself
   V.5   5 *targes of proof* shields of proved strength   7 *grace* favor

9   Such precious deeds in one that promised nought
10   But beggary and poor looks.
     CYMBELINE   No tidings of him?
     PISANIO
       He hath been searched among the dead and living,
       But no trace of him.
     CYMBELINE   To my grief, I am
       The heir of his reward,   *[To Belarius, Guiderius, and*
          Arviragus] which I will add
14   To you, the liver, heart, and brain of Britain,
15   By whom I grant she lives. 'Tis now the time
       To ask of whence you are. Report it.
     BELARIUS   Sir,
       In Cambria are we born, and gentlemen.
       Further to boast were neither true nor modest,
       Unless I add we are honest.
     CYMBELINE   Bow your knees.
20   Arise my knights o' th' battle; I create you
21   Companions to our person and will fit you
22   With dignities becoming your estates.
          Enter Cornelius and Ladies.
23   There's business in these faces. Why so sadly
       Greet you our victory? You look like Romans
       And not o' th' court of Britain.
     CORNELIUS   Hail, great king!
       To sour your happiness I must report
27   The queen is dead.
     CYMBELINE   Who worse than a physician
       Would this report become? But I consider
       By med'cine life may be prolonged, yet death
30   Will seize the doctor too. How ended she?

---

9 *promised* offered, presented   **14** *the liver . . . brain* who are the vital parts
15 *she* Britain   **20** *knights . . . battle* knights created on the battlefield (cf.
"battlefield commission")   **21** *fit* equip   **22** *estates* status as knights   **23**
There's . . . faces i.e., their looks show that these persons have something important to tell   **27** *Who* (for "whom")

CORNELIUS
    With horror, madly dying, like her life,
    Which, being cruel to the world, concluded
    Most cruel to herself. What she confessed
    I will report, so please you. These her women
    Can trip me if I err, who with wet cheeks   36
    Were present when she finished.
CYMBELINE   Prithee say.
CORNELIUS
    First, she confessed she never loved you, only
    Affected greatness got by you, not you;   39
    Married your royalty, was wife to your place,   40
    Abhorred your person.
CYMBELINE   She alone knew this,
    And but she spoke it dying, I would not   42
    Believe her lips in opening it. Proceed.   43
CORNELIUS
    Your daughter, whom she bore in hand to love   44
    With such integrity, she did confess
    Was as a scorpion to her sight, whose life,
    But that her flight prevented it, she had
    Ta'en off by poison.   48
CYMBELINE   O most delicate fiend!
    Who is't can read a woman? Is there more?
CORNELIUS
    More, sir, and worse. She did confess she had   50
    For you a mortal mineral, which, being took,   51
    Should by the minute feed on life and, ling'ring,   52
    By inches waste you. In which time she purposed,   53
    By watching, weeping, tendance, kissing, to   54
    O'ercome you with her show and, in time,   55

---

36 *trip me* point out my mistake   39 *Affected* desired, loved   42 *but* but for
the fact that   43 *opening* disclosing   44 *bore in hand* pretended   48 *Ta'en
off* destroyed; *delicate* subtle   51 *mortal mineral* deadly poison   52 *by the
minute* minute by minute   53 *waste* consume, destroy   54 *tendance* atten-
tiveness   55 *show* pretense (of devotion)

56   When she had fitted you with her craft, to work
57   Her son into th' adoption of the crown;
      But failing of her end by his strange absence,
      Grew shameless desperate, opened, in despite
60   Of heaven and men, her purposes, repented
      The evils she hatched were not effected, so
      Despairing died.
CYMBELINE   Heard you all this, her women?
LADY
      We did, so please your highness.
CYMBELINE   Mine eyes
      Were not in fault, for she was beautiful,
      Mine ears, that heard her flattery, nor my heart,
66   That thought her like her seeming. It had been vicious
      To have mistrusted her. Yet, O my daughter,
68   That it was folly in me thou mayst say,
69   And prove it in thy feeling. Heaven mend all!
          Enter Lucius, Iachimo, [the Soothsayer,] and other
          Roman Prisoners, [Posthumus] Leonatus behind, and
          Imogen [and Briton soldiers guarding them].
70   Thou com'st not, Caius, now for tribute. That
71   The Britons have razed out, though with the loss
      Of many a bold one, whose kinsmen have made suit
73   That their good souls may be appeased with slaughter
      Of you their captives, which ourself have granted.
75   So think of your estate.
LUCIUS
      Consider, sir, the chance of war. The day
77   Was yours by accident; had it gone with us,
      We should not, when the blood was cool, have threatened
      Our prisoners with the sword. But since the gods
80   Will have it thus, that nothing but our lives

---

56 *fitted* shaped to her purpose   57 *adoption of* adoption by you as heir to
60 *repented* was bitterly sorry because   66 *seeming* appearance; *had been vicious* would have been a fault   68 *it* i.e., trusting her   69 *prove* experience; *feeling* suffering   71 *razed out* erased   73 *their* i.e., of those lost in battle
75 *estate* spiritual state (i.e., prepare for death)   77 *had . . . us* had we won

May be called ransom, let it come. Sufficeth
A Roman with a Roman's heart can suffer.
Augustus lives to think on't – and so much
For my peculiar care. This one thing only   84
I will entreat: my boy, a Briton born,
Let him be ransomed. Never master had
A page so kind, so duteous, diligent,
So tender over his occasions, true,   88
So feat, so nurselike. Let his virtue join   89
With my request, which I'll make bold your highness   90
Cannot deny. He hath done no Briton harm,
Though he have served a Roman. Save him, sir,
And spare no blood beside.   93
CYMBELINE   I have surely seen him;
His favor is familiar to me. Boy,   94
Thou hast looked thyself into my grace   95
And art mine own. I know not why, wherefore,   96
To say "Live, boy." Ne'er thank thy master. Live,
And ask of Cymbeline what boon thou wilt,
Fitting my bounty and thy state; I'll give it,   99
Yea, though thou do demand a prisoner,   100
The noblest ta'en.
IMOGEN   I humbly thank your highness.
LUCIUS
I do not bid thee beg my life, good lad,
And yet I know thou wilt.
IMOGEN   No, no, alack,
There's other work in hand. I see a thing   104
Bitter to me as death; your life, good master,
Must shuffle for itself.   106

---

84 *my peculiar care* care for myself   88 *tender . . . occasions* sensitive to his (master's) needs   89 *feat* skillful   93 *no blood beside* the blood of no one else   94 *favor* face   95 *looked . . . grace* by your looks secured my favor   96 *I . . . wherefore* (cf. "I don't know why I'm doing it"; hence, "You need not thank Lucius")   99 *Fitting* appropriate to   104 *thing* (cf. ll. 138–39)   106 *shuffle* make out as best it can

LUCIUS   The boy disdains me;
107   He leaves me, scorns me. Briefly die their joys
108   That place them on the truth of girls and boys.
109   Why stands he so perplexed?
CYMBELINE   What wouldst thou, boy?
110   I love thee more and more. Think more and more
       What's best to ask. Know'st him thou look'st on? Speak.
       Wilt have him live? Is he thy kin? Thy friend?
IMOGEN
       He is a Roman, no more kin to me
       Than I to your highness; who, being born your vassal,
115   Am something nearer.
CYMBELINE   Wherefore ey'st him so?
IMOGEN
       I'll tell you, sir, in private, if you please
       To give me hearing.
CYMBELINE   Ay, with all my heart,
       And lend my best attention. What's thy name?
IMOGEN
       Fidele, sir.
120 CYMBELINE   Thou'rt my good youth, my page;
       I'll be thy master. Walk with me; speak freely.
          [Cymbeline and Imogen talk apart.]
BELARIUS
       Is not this boy revived from death?
ARVIRAGUS   One sand another
123   Not more resembles that sweet rosy lad
       Who died, and was Fidele. What think you?
GUIDERIUS
       The same dead thing alive.
BELARIUS
       Peace, peace, see further. He eyes us not; forbear.

_____

107 *Briefly* soon 107–8 *their joys / That* the joys of those who 108
place . . . truth make them depend on the fidelity 109 *perplexed* troubled
115 *something nearer* somewhat closer (to you than he is to me) 123
Not . . . lad (unusually elliptical; some words may be lost)

Creatures may be alike. Were't he, I am sure
He would have spoke to us.   128
GUIDERIUS   But we see him dead.
BELARIUS
Be silent; let's see further.
PISANIO   *[Aside]*   It is my mistress.
Since she is living, let the time run on   130
To good or bad.
    [Cymbeline and Imogen come forward.]
CYMBELINE   *[To Imogen]*   Come, stand thou by our side;
Make thy demand aloud. *[To Iachimo]* Sir, step you forth,
Give answer to this boy, and do it freely;
Or, by our greatness and the grace of it,   134
Which is our honor, bitter torture shall
Winnow the truth from falsehood. – On, speak to him.
IMOGEN
My boon is that this gentleman may render   137
Of whom he had this ring.
POSTHUMUS   *[Aside]*   What's that to him?
CYMBELINE
That diamond upon your finger, say
How came it yours.   140
IACHIMO
Thou'lt torture me to leave unspoken that   141
Which to be spoke would torture thee.
CYMBELINE   .   How? Me?
IACHIMO
I am glad to be constrained to utter that
Which torments me to conceal. By villainy
I got this ring. 'Twas Leonatus' jewel,
Whom thou didst banish, and – which more may grieve
    thee,
As it doth me – a nobler sir ne'er lived
'Twixt sky and ground. Wilt thou hear more, my lord?

---

128 *see* saw   134–35 *the grace . . . honor* our honor, which embellishes (our
greatness)   137 *render* tell   141 *to leave* for leaving

CYMBELINE

150   All that belongs to this.

IACHIMO   That paragon, thy daughter,
For whom my heart drops blood and my false spirits
Quail to remember – Give me leave; I faint.

CYMBELINE
. My daughter? What of her? Renew thy strength.

154   I had rather thou shouldst live while nature will
Than die ere I hear more. Strive, man, and speak.

IACHIMO
Upon a time – unhappy was the clock
That struck the hour! – it was in Rome – accursed
The mansion where! – 'twas at a feast – O, would
Our viands had been poisoned, or at least

160   Those which I heaved to head! – the good Posthumus –
What should I say? He was too good to be
Where ill men were, and was the best of all
Amongst the rar'st of good ones – sitting sadly,
Hearing us praise our loves of Italy

165   For beauty that made barren the swelled boast
166   Of him that best could speak; for feature, laming
167   The shrine of Venus or straight-pitched Minerva,
168   Postures beyond brief nature; for condition,
169   A shop of all the qualities that man
170   Loves woman for; besides that hook of wiving,
Fairness which strikes the eye –

CYMBELINE   I stand on fire.

172·   Come to the matter.

IACHIMO   All too soon I shall,
Unless thou wouldst grieve quickly. This Posthumus,

---

154 *while nature will* i.e., your natural life   160 *heaved to head* raised to
mouth   165 *made . . . boast* rendered even an exaggerated boast powerless
(to express)   166 *feature* figure; *laming* making a cripple of   167 *shrine*
image; *straight-pitched* erect   168 *Postures* forms; *beyond brief nature* of immortal beings, more enduring (as art) than natural beings; *condition* character   169 *shop* store   170 *hook* fishhook (i.e., bait); *of wiving* for marriage
172 *matter* point

Most like a noble lord in love and one
That had a royal lover, took his hint,   175
And not dispraising whom we praised – therein
He was as calm as virtue – he began
His mistress' picture; which by his tongue being made,
And then a mind put in't, either our brags   179
Were cracked of kitchen trulls, or his description   180
Proved us unspeaking sots.   181
CYMBELINE   Nay, nay, to th' purpose.
IACHIMO
Your daughter's chastity – there it begins.
He spake of her as Dian had hot dreams   183
And she alone were cold; whereat I, wretch,   184
Made scruple of his praise and wagered with him   185
Pieces of gold 'gainst this which then he wore
Upon his honored finger, to attain
In suit the place of's bed and win this ring   188
By hers and mine adultery. He, true knight,
No lesser of her honor confident   190
Than I did truly find her, stakes this ring;
And would so, had it been a carbuncle   192
Of Phoebus' wheel, and might so safely, had it   193
Been all the worth of's car. Away to Britain
Post I in this design. Well may you, sir,   195
Remember me at court, where I was taught
Of your chaste daughter the wide difference   197
'Twixt amorous and villainous. Being thus quenched   198
Of hope, not longing, mine Italian brain

---

175 *lover* woman in love with him; *hint* opportunity   179 *mind put in't* i.e.,
she had brains as well as beauty   180 *cracked of* boasted about; *trulls*
wenches   181 *unspeaking sots* inarticulate fools; *to th' purpose* (keep) to the
point   183 *as* as if; *hot* lecherous   184 *cold* chaste   185 *Made scruple of*
stated disbelief in   188 *In suit* by wooing   192 *would so* would have done
so; *carbuncle* probably "ruby"   193 *Phoebus' wheel* i.e., wheel on the sun's
chariot; *might so* might have done so   195 *Post* hurry   197 *Of* by   198
amorous faithful love   198–99 *quenched / Of* cooled off in

200   Gan in your duller Britain operate
201   Most vilely; for my vantage, excellent.
202   And, to be brief, my practice so prevailed
203   That I returned with simular proof enough
       To make the noble Leonatus mad
205   By wounding his belief in her renown
206   With tokens thus and thus; averring notes
       Of chamber hanging, pictures, this her bracelet –
       O cunning, how I got it! – nay, some marks
       Of secret on her person, that he could not
210   But think her bond of chastity quite cracked,
211   I having ta'en the forfeit. Whereupon –
       Methinks I see him now –
       POSTHUMUS   [Advancing]   Ay, so thou dost,
       Italian fiend! Ay me, most credulous fool,
214   Egregious murderer, thief, anything
       That's due to all the villains past, in being,
       To come! O, give me cord or knife or poison,
217   Some upright justicer! Thou, king, send out
       For torturers ingenious. It is I
219   That all th' abhorrèd things o' th' earth amend
220   By being worse than they. I am Posthumus,
       That killed thy daughter – villainlike, I lie –
       That caused a lesser villain than myself,
       A sacrilegious thief, to do't. The temple
224   Of virtue was she; yea, and she herself.
       Spit, and throw stones, cast mire upon me, set
       The dogs o' th' street to bay me; every villain
       Be called Posthumus Leonatus, and
228   Be villainy less than 'twas! O Imogen!

---

200 *duller Britain* (northern countries supposedly produced slower minds)
201 *vantage* profit   **202** *practice* scheming   **203** *simular* simulated   **205**
renown good name   **206** *averring notes* affirming the marks   **210** *cracked*
broken   **211** *ta'en the forfeit* gained what was forfeited (by breach of bond)
214 *anything* i.e., any name   **217** *justicer* judge   **219** *amend* make (seem)
better   **224** *she herself* virtue herself   **228** *Be . . . 'twas* i.e., I have made
other villainies seem smaller

My queen, my life, my wife! O Imogen,
Imogen, Imogen!   *230*
IMOGEN   Peace, my lord. Hear, hear –
POSTHUMUS
   Shall's have a play of this? Thou scornful page,   231
   There lie thy part.   232
         [Pushes her away; she falls.]
PISANIO   O gentlemen, help!
   Mine and your mistress! O my lord Posthumus,
   You ne'er killed Imogen till now. Help, help!
   Mine honored lady!
CYMBELINE   Does the world go round?
POSTHUMUS
   How come these staggers on me?   236
PISANIO   Wake, my mistress!
CYMBELINE
   If this be so, the gods do mean to strike me
   To death with mortal joy.   238
PISANIO   How fares my mistress?
IMOGEN
   O, get thee from my sight;
   Thou gav'st me poison. Dangerous fellow, hence;   *240*
   Breathe not where princes are.   241
CYMBELINE   The tune of Imogen!
PISANIO
   Lady,
   The gods throw stones of sulphur on me if   243
   That box I gave you was not thought by me
   A precious thing; I had it from the queen.   245
CYMBELINE
   New matter still.   246
IMOGEN   It poisoned me.

---

231 *Shall's* shall us – i.e., we 232 *There . . . part* lying there is your role
236 *these staggers* this dizziness, agitation 238 *mortal* fatal 241 *tune* voice
243 *stones of sulphur* thunderbolts 245 *precious* beneficial 246 *matter* de-
velopments

CORNELIUS   O gods!
      I left out one thing which the queen confessed,
248   Which must approve thee honest. "If Pisanio
249   Have," said she, "given his mistress that confection
250   Which I gave him for cordial, she is served
      As I would serve a rat."
      CYMBELINE   What's this, Cornelius?
      CORNELIUS
      The queen, sir, very oft importuned me
253   To temper poisons for her, still pretending
      The satisfaction of her knowledge only
      In killing creatures vile, as cats and dogs
256   Of no esteem. I, dreading that her purpose
257   Was of more danger, did compound for her
258   A certain stuff which, being ta'en, would cease
      The present pow'r of life, but in short time
260   All offices of nature should again
      Do their due functions. Have you ta'en of it?
      IMOGEN
262   Most like I did, for I was dead.
      BELARIUS   My boys,
      There was our error.
      GUIDERIUS   This is sure Fidele.
      IMOGEN
      Why did you throw your wedded lady from you?
265   Think that you are upon a rock, and now
266   Throw me again.
            [Embraces him.]
      POSTHUMUS   Hang there like fruit, my soul,
      Till the tree die!

---

248 *approve* prove; *honest* truthful   249 *confection* mixture   253 *temper*
mix; *pretending* alleging as her purpose   256 *esteem* value   257 *of more danger* more harmful   258 *cease* cut off   260 *offices of nature* bodily parts   262
like probably; *dead* as if dead   265 *rock* i.e., firm ground (?) (sometimes
emended to "lock" and explained as a metaphor from wrestling)   266
Throw me again i.e., if you can (we are now inseparable)

CYMBELINE   How now, my flesh, my child?
  What, mak'st thou me a dullard in this act?   268
  Wilt thou not speak to me?
IMOGEN   *[Kneeling]*   Your blessing, sir.
BELARIUS   *[To Guiderius and Arviragus]*
  Though you did love this youth, I blame ye not;   270
  You had a motive for't.   271
CYMBELINE   My tears that fall
  Prove holy water on thee. Imogen,
  Thy mother's dead.
IMOGEN   I am sorry for't, my lord.
CYMBELINE
  O, she was naught, and long of her it was   274
  That we meet here so strangely; but her son
  Is gone, we know not how nor where.
PISANIO   My lord,
  Now fear is from me, I'll speak truth. Lord Cloten,
  Upon my lady's missing, came to me
  With his sword drawn, foamed at the mouth, and swore,
  If I discovered not which way she was gone,   280
  It was my instant death. By accident
  I had a feignèd letter of my master's   282
  Then in my pocket, which directed him
  To seek her on the mountains near to Milford;
  Where, in a frenzy, in my master's garments,
  Which he enforced from me, away he posts
  With unchaste purpose and with oath to violate
  My lady's honor. What became of him
  I further know not
GUIDERIUS   Let me end the story:
  I slew him there.   290

---

268 *dullard* i.e., by ignoring me (and giving me no lines to speak); *act* perhaps, play (cf. ll. 231–32) **271** *motive* cause **274** *naught* evil; *long of* because of **280** *discovered* revealed **282** *letter* (cf. III 5.99–100) **290** *forfend* forbid

CYMBELINE   Marry, the gods forfend!
291   I would not thy good deeds should from my lips
       Pluck a hard sentence. Prithee, valiant youth,
293   Deny't again.
GUIDERIUS   I have spoke it, and I did it.
CYMBELINE
       He was a prince.
GUIDERIUS
       A most incivil one. The wrongs he did me
       Were nothing princelike, for he did provoke me
       With language that would make me spurn the sea
       If it could so roar to me. I cut off's head,
       And am right glad he is not standing here
300   To tell this tale of mine.
CYMBELINE   I am sorrow for thee.
       By thine own tongue thou art condemned and must
       Endure our law. Thou'rt dead.
IMOGEN   That headless man
       I thought had been my lord.
CYMBELINE   Bind the offender
       And take him from our presence.
BELARIUS   Stay, sir king.
       This man is better than the man he slew,
       As well descended as thyself, and hath
       More of thee merited than a band of Clotens
308   Had ever scar for. Let his arms alone;
       They were not born for bondage.
CYMBELINE   Why, old soldier,
310   Wilt thou undo the worth thou art unpaid for
       By tasting of our wrath? How of descent
       As good as we?

---

291 *thy good deeds* (that after) thy good deeds (against the Romans, thou)
293 *again* what you have just said   300 *tell . . . mine* i.e., report that he cut
off my head; *sorrow* (a possible idiom; some editors emend to "sorry")   308
Had . . . for earned by battle wounds

ARVIRAGUS   In that he spake too far.
CYMBELINE
And thou shalt die for't.   313
BELARIUS   We will die all three
But I will prove that two on's are as good   314
As I have given out him. My sons, I must
For mine own part unfold a dangerous speech,   316
Though haply well for you.
ARVIRAGUS   Your danger's ours.
GUIDERIUS
And our good his.   318
BELARIUS   Have at it then. By leave,
Thou hadst, great king, a subject who
Was called Belarius.   320
CYMBELINE   What of him? He is
A banished traitor.
BELARIUS   He it is that hath
Assumed this age; indeed a banished man,   322
I know not how a traitor.
CYMBELINE   Take him hence.
The whole world shall not save him.   324
BELARIUS   Not too hot.
First pay me for the nursing of thy sons,
And let it be confiscate all, so soon   326
As I have received it.
CYMBELINE   Nursing of my sons?
BELARIUS
I am too blunt and saucy; here's my knee.   328
Ere I arise I will prefer my sons;   329
Then spare not the old father. Mighty sir,   330
These two young gentlemen that call me father

---

313 *thou* i.e., Belarius   314 *But* unless; *on's* of us   316 *For . . . speech* make
an explanatory statement dangerous to myself   318 *Have at it* let's go ahead;
By leave by your permission   322 *Assumed this age* taken on this look of age
324 *hot* hasty   326 *it* the payment   328 *saucy* direct, "fresh"   329 *prefer* advance

And think they are my sons are none of mine;
They are the issue of your loins, my liege,
And blood of your begetting.
CYMBELINE   How? My issue?
BELARIUS
   So sure as you your father's. I, old Morgan,
336   Am that Belarius whom you sometime banished.
337   Your pleasure was my mere offense, my punishment
   Itself, and all my treason; that I suffered
   Was all the harm I did. These gentle princes –
340   For such and so they are – these twenty years
341   Have I trained up; those arts they have as I
   Could put into them. My breeding was, sir, as
   Your highness knows. Their nurse, Euriphile,
   Whom for the theft I wedded, stole these children
345   Upon my banishment. I moved her to't,
   Having received the punishment before
347   For that which I did then. Beaten for loyalty
   Excited me to treason. Their dear loss,
349   The more of you 'twas felt, the more it shaped
350   Unto my end of stealing them. But, gracious sir,
   Here are your sons again, and I must lose
   Two of the sweet'st companions in the world.
   The benediction of these covering heavens
   Fall on their heads like dew, for they are worthy
   To inlay heaven with stars.
CYMBELINE   Thou weep'st and speak'st.
356   The service that you three have done is more
357   Unlike than this thou tell'st. I lost my children;
   If these be they, I know not how to wish
   A pair of worthier sons.

---

336 *sometime* once · 337–38 *Your . . . treason* my whole offense, etc., existed
only because it pleased you (to declare them)   341 *arts* accomplishments
345 *moved* incited   347 *Beaten* being beaten   349 *of* by   349–50
shaped . . . of served my end in   356 *service* i.e., in battle   357 *Unlike*
improbable

BELARIUS   Be pleased awhile.
 This gentleman whom I call Polydore,   *360*
 Most worthy prince, as yours, is true Guiderius;
 This gentleman, my Cadwal, Arviragus,
 Your younger princely son. He, sir, was lapped   *363*
 In a most curious mantle, wrought by th' hand   *364*
 Of his queen mother, which for more probation   *365*
 I can with ease produce.
CYMBELINE   Guiderius had
 Upon his neck a mole, a sanguine star;   *367*
 It was a mark of wonder.
BELARIUS   This is he,
 Who hath upon him still that natural stamp.
 It was wise Nature's end in the donation   *370*
 To be his evidence now.   *371*
CYMBELINE   O, what am I?
 A mother to the birth of three? Ne'er mother
 Rejoiced deliverance more. Blessed pray you be,
 That, after this strange starting from your orbs,   *374*
 You may reign in them now! O Imogen,
 Thou hast lost by this a kingdom.
IMOGEN   No, my lord,
 I have got two worlds by't. O my gentle brothers,
 Have we thus met? O, never say hereafter
 But I am truest speaker. You called me brother
 When I was but your sister, I you brothers   *380*
 When ye were so indeed.
CYMBELINE   Did you e'er meet?
ARVIRAGUS
 Ay, my good lord.
GUIDERIUS   And at first meeting loved,
 Continued so until we thought he died.

---

363 *lapped* wrapped 364 *curious* artfully wrought 365 *probation* proof
367 *sanguine* blood-red 370 *end* purpose; *donation* endowing (him with
the mark) 371 *his evidence* evidence of his identity 374 *orbs* orbits

CORNELIUS
   By the queen's dram she swallowed.
CYMBELINE   O rare instinct!
385   When shall I hear all through? This fierce abridgment
386   Hath to it circumstantial branches, which
   Distinction should be rich in. Where, how lived you?
   And when came you to serve our Roman captive?
   How parted with your brothers? How first met them?
390   Why fled you from the court? And whither? These,
391   And your three motives to the battle, with
   I know not how much more, should be demanded,
393   And all the other by-dependences
394   From chance to chance; but nor the time nor place
395   Will serve our long interrogatories. See,
   Posthumus anchors upon Imogen,
   And she like harmless lightning throws her eye
   On him, her brothers, me, her master, hitting
399   Each object with a joy; the counterchange
400   Is severally in all. Let's quit this ground
401   And smoke the temple with our sacrifices.
      [To Belarius]
402   Thou art my brother; so we'll hold thee ever.
IMOGEN
403   You are my father too, and did relieve me
404   To see this gracious season.
CYMBELINE   All o'erjoyed
   Save these in bonds; let them be joyful too,
406   For they shall taste our comfort.

---

385 *fierce abridgment* hugely compressed account   386 *branches* ramifications, details   386–87 *which . . . in* which, as they are distinguished, should be plentiful   391 *your three motives* what impelled you three   393 *by-dependences* related matters   394 *chance* happening   395 *Will serve* are suited to   399 *counterchange* exchange   400 *Is . . . all* i.e., all engage in it, each according to his/her relationship to the others   401 *smoke* fill with incense   402 *hold* regard   403 *You* i.e., Belarius; *relieve* aid   404 *gracious season* joyful occasion   406 *taste our comfort* share in our well-being

IMOGEN   My good master,
  I will yet do you service.
LUCIUS   Happy be you!
CYMBELINE
  The forlorn soldier, that so nobly fought,   408
  He would have well becomed this place and graced
  The thankings of a king.   *410*
POSTHUMUS   I am, sir,
  The soldier that did company these three
  In poor beseeming; 'twas a fitment for   412
  The purpose I then followed. That I was he,   413
  Speak, Iachimo. I had you down and might
  Have made you finish.   415
IACHIMO *[Kneeling]*   I am down again,
  But now my heavy conscience sinks my knee,   416
  And then your force did. Take that life, beseech you,
  Which I so often owe; but your ring first,   418
  And here the bracelet of the truest princess
  That ever swore her faith.   *420*
POSTHUMUS   Kneel not to me.
  The pow'r that I have on you is to spare you;
  The malice towards you to forgive you. Live,
  And deal with others better.   423
CYMBELINE   Nobly doomed!
  We'll learn our freeness of a son-in-law: 424
  Pardon's the word to all.
ARVIRAGUS   *[To Posthumus]* You holp us, sir,
  As you did mean indeed to be our brother.
  Joyed are we that you are.   427
POSTHUMUS
  Your servant, princes. Good my lord of Rome,

---

408 *forlorn* missing **412** *beseeming* appearance (i.e., garb); *fitment for* garb
fitted for **413** *followed* was carrying out **415** *finish* die **416** *sinks* makes
bend **418** *often* many times (because of the extent of my misdeeds) **423**
doomed judged **424** *freeness* generosity **427** *you are* i.e., our brother

Call forth your soothsayer. As I slept, methought
430   Great Jupiter, upon his eagle backed,
431   Appeared to me, with other spritely shows
       Of mine own kindred. When I waked, I found
433   This label on my bosom, whose containing
434   Is so from sense in hardness that I can
435   Make no collection of it. Let him show
436   His skill in the construction.

LUCIUS   Philarmonus!

SOOTHSAYER
       Here, my good lord.

LUCIUS   Read, and declare the meaning.

SOOTHSAYER *[Reads.]* "When as a lion's whelp shall, to
       himself unknown, without seeking find, and be em-
440   braced by a piece of tender air; and when from a stately
       cedar shall be lopped branches which, being dead many
       years, shall after revive, be jointed to the old stock, and
       freshly grow; then shall Posthumus end his miseries,
       Britain be fortunate and flourish in peace and plenty."
       [To Leonatus]
       Thou, Leonatus, art the lion's whelp;
       The fit and apt construction of thy name,
447   Being *Leo-natus,* doth import so much.
       [To Cymbeline]
       The piece of tender air, thy virtuous daughter,
449   Which we call *mollis aer,* and *mollis aer*
450   We term it *mulier;* which *mulier* I divine
       Is this most constant wife, who even now
452   Answering the letter of the oracle,
       [To Posthumus]

---

430 *upon . . . backed* on the back of his eagle   431 *spritely shows* ghostly vi-
sions   433 *label* piece of paper; *containing* contents   434 *from . . . hardness*
hard to understand   435 *collection* elucidation   436 *construction* constru-
ing, interpreting (of it)   447 *Leo-natus* lion-born; *import* mean, imply   449
mollis aer tender air (a supposed origin of *mulier,* woman)   452 *Answering*
according to

Unknown to you, unsought, were clipped about   453
With this most tender air.   454
CYMBELINE   This hath some seeming.
SOOTHSAYER
The lofty cedar, royal Cymbeline,
Personates thee, and thy lopped branches point   456
Thy two sons forth; who, by Belarius stol'n,
For many years thought dead, are now revived,
To the majestic cedar joined, whose issue   459
Promises Britain peace and plenty.   *460*
CYMBELINE   Well,
My peace we will begin. And, Caius Lucius,
Although the victor, we submit to Caesar
And to the Roman empire, promising
To pay our wonted tribute, from the which
We were dissuaded by our wicked queen,
Whom heavens in justice, both on her and hers,   466
Have laid most heavy hand.
SOOTHSAYER
The fingers of the pow'rs above do tune
The harmony of this peace. The vision   469
Which I made known to Lucius ere the stroke   *470*
Of this yet scarce-cold battle, at this instant
Is full accomplished; for the Roman eagle,
From south to west on wing soaring aloft,
Lessened herself and in the beams o' th' sun
So vanished; which foreshowed our princely eagle,
Th' imperial Caesar, should again unite
His favor with the radiant Cymbeline,
Which shines here in the west.   478
CYMBELINE   Laud we the gods,
And let our crooked smokes climb to their nostrils   479

---

453 *were clipped about* i.e., you were embraced (the passage is grammatically incoherent) 454 *seeming* plausibility 456 *Personates* stands for 456–57 *point . . . forth* indicate your two sons 459 *issue* descendants 466 *Whom* on whom; *hers* i.e., Cloten 469 *vision* (cf. IV.2.346 ff.) 478 *Laud* praise 479 *crooked* curling

480 From our blessed altars. Publish we this peace
481 To all our subjects. Set we forward; let
A Roman and a British ensign wave
Friendly together. So through Lud's town march,
And in the temple of great Jupiter
Our peace we'll ratify, seal it with feasts.
486 Set on there! Never was a war did cease,
Ere bloody hands were washed, with such a peace.

Exeunt.

---

481 *Set we forward* let us march   **486** *Set on there* forward march

FOR THE BEST IN PAPERBACKS, LOOK FOR THE

The distinguished Pelican Shakespeare series, newly revised
to be the premier choice for students, professors, and
general readers well into the 21st century

All's Well That Ends Well
ISBN 0-14-071460-X

Antony and Cleopatra
ISBN 0-14-071452-9

As You Like It
ISBN 0-14-071471-5

The Comedy of Errors
ISBN 0-14-071474-X

Coriolanus
ISBN 0-14-071473-1

Cymbeline
ISBN 0-14-071472-3

Hamlet
ISBN 0-14-071454-5

Henry IV, Part 1
ISBN 0-14-071456-1

Henry IV, Part 2
ISBN 0-14-071457-X

Henry V
ISBN 0-14-071458-8

Henry VI, Part 1
ISBN 0-14-071465-0

Henry VI, Part 2
ISBN 0-14-071466-9

Henry VI, Part 3
ISBN 0-14-071467-7

Henry VIII
ISBN 0-14-071475-8

Julius Caesar
ISBN 0-14-071468-5

King John
ISBN 0-14-071459-6

King Lear
ISBN 0-14-071476-6

King Lear (The Quarto and Folio Texts)
ISBN 0-14-071490-1

Love's Labor's Lost
ISBN 0-14-071477-4

Macbeth
ISBN 0-14-071478-2

Measure for Measure
ISBN 0-14-071479-0

The Merchant of Venice
ISBN 0-14-071462-6

The Merry Wives of Windsor
ISBN 0-14-071464-2

A Midsummer Night's Dream
ISBN 0-14-071455-3

Much Ado About Nothing
ISBN 0-14-071480-4

The Narrative Poems
ISBN 0-14-071481-2

Othello
ISBN 0-14-071463-4

Pericles
ISBN 0-14-071469-3

Richard II
ISBN 0-14-071482-0

Richard III
ISBN 0-14-071483-9

Romeo and Juliet
ISBN 0-14-071484-7

The Sonnets
ISBN 0-14-071453-7

The Taming of the Shrew
ISBN 0-14-071451-0

The Tempest
ISBN 0-14-071485-5

Timon of Athens
ISBN 0-14-071487-1

Titus Andronicus
ISBN 0-14-071491-X

Troilus and Cressida
ISBN 0-14-071486-3

Twelfth Night
ISBN 0-14-071489-8

The Two Gentlemen of Verona
ISBN 0-14-071461-8

The Winter's Tale
ISBN 0-14-071488-X